CONTEMPORARY CHRISTIAN STUDIES
EDITOR: PAUL AVIS

CHRISTIAN THEOLOGY AND WORLD
RELIGIONS:
A GLOBAL APPROACH

CHRISTIAN THEOLOGY AND WORLD RELIGIONS

A Global Approach

FRANK WHALING

Marshall Pickering

Marshall Morgan and Scott
Marshall Pickering
3 Beggarwood Lane, Basingstoke, Hants RG23 7LP, UK

Copyright © 1986 by Frank Whaling

First published in 1986 by Marshall Morgan and Scott Publications Ltd
Part of the Marshall Pickering Holdings Group
A subsidary of the Zondervan Corporation

ISBN: 0 551 01336 2

Phototypeset in Linotron Baskerville
by Input Typesetting Ltd, London.

Printed in Great Britain by Camelot Press Ltd, Southampton.

To My Wife Patricia
My Son John Prem Francis
My Daughter Ruth Shanti Patricia

CONTENTS

PREFACE

The engagement of Christian theology with the religious traditions of our world is not just *a* crucial part but probably *the* crucial part of her task in the global context in which we live. This is the sustained theme of this book. It is pursued from first page to last under many headings and with the use of many variations.

Underlying, although not dominating the discussion is our global situation itself: our need as a human race to think globally or possibly perish. Any discussion of our global context must include mention of not only our natural resources and the threat to our natural environment, and our human resources and the threat to our humane future, but also of our spiritual resources and the threat to our spiritual future. The corollary may also be the case—that what appears to be a series of threats may in fact be a congeries of glorious opportunities to overcome our past parochial preoccupations in order to construct under God a global future of exhilarating promise for the human race. This global perspective, therefore, is the framework within which our more detailed discussion of Christian theology and world religions takes place.

Within the main theme there appear a number of important sub-themes: What is theology? What is Christian theology? What is Religious Studies and how do world religions fit into this area of thought? How can we understand world religions? What are the possible Christian theological attitudes to other religions? How can Christian theology renew itself through world religions? How can the Christian theological engagement with other religions prepare for a future global Christian systematic theology? These are some of the important variations within this comprehensive treatment of the overarching topic of Christian theology and world religions.

For historical reasons, the engagement with world religions has been undervalued within Christian theology. By reason of lack of knowledge or lack of training or both, there is often a certain nervousness about this topic among Christian theologians, clergy and laymen at the same time as there is an alarmed awareness that it is a subject of mind-boggling yet very practical importance. The time for reticence about this area of thought is passing if it has not already past. The issues are far too important for timidity of any sort. It is vital that any serious-minded Christian alive today should become informed about this area of concern. It is inevitable, in a global world, that it can only grow in significance during the years that are to come.

This book gives an overview of all the main issues involved within the umbrella topic of CHRISTIAN THEOLOGY AND WORLD RELIGIONS. It offers an imaginative challenge to the reader to become involved in heart as well as in mind to the end that his or her Christian theological vision may revolve around a wider axis after reflective grappling with these pages.

As this is a book on Christian theology rather than a technical work on world religions, I have avoided diacritical marks and the complicated apparatus of technical niceties when using words from other religious traditions. For example the reader will find reference to Krishna instead of (the more technically correct) Kṛṣṇa, Vishnu instead of Viṣṇu, Koran instead of Qur'ān, and so on. I apologise to fellow experts in world religions but feel that they will understand that ease of understanding is more important in this instance than technical purity.

For the first time I have also used inclusive language in this work. Reference will therefore be made to humanity, humankind, persons, etc, rather than to man or men when talking about people in general.

I am deeply grateful to a number of institutions and persons for their help in fashioning this book. To Douglas Grant of the Scottish Academic Press, and the Editors of the Scottish Journal of Theology, I offer my thanks for permission to adapt and use material from the Scottish Journal of Theology, volumes 32 and 34, on 'The Trinity and the Structure of

Religious Life' and 'The Development of the Word
"Theology" '. I thank Rev. Deryck Dugmore, and Rev. Dr.
Jan Dijkman, the Editors of Religious Education, for
permission to adapt and use part of my essay on 'Christianity
and African Religions' from Volume 42 of Religious
Education. I am grateful for their comments to my colleagues
at the Institute for Research into World Religions at the
Chinese Academy of Social Sciences in Beijing, China, to
whom I first delivered as a paper my piece in chapter two on
'A Historical Interpretation of Human Religiousness', and I
am equally grateful to my co-Fulbright Fellows at Harvard
with whom I discussed the analyses of the global situation
scattered throughout this work.

Thanks are due to Mrs Frances Anderson of Edinburgh
who typed this manuscript. It is my privilege to record thanks
to Brenda Watson and Edward Hulmes, Director and former
Director of the Farmington Institute Oxford, and to E. R.
('Bobby') Wills, the President of the Farmington Trust and
Institute, for our work on the Edinburgh/Farmington Project
of which this book is in part a fruit. Last but not least I am
deeply grateful to John Hunt and Debbie Thorpe of Marshalls
and to Rev. Dr. Paul Avis, the Editor of this series, whose
patience and concern in the production of this book I will
never forget.

Finally and uniquely I pay tribute to my wife Patricia, and
my children John Prem Francis and Ruth Shanti Patricia, for
being themselves and I am happy to dedicate this book to
them.

CHAPTER ONE

INTRODUCTION

The time is long past when Christians and Christian theologians could afford to ignore the data and world views of the other religious traditions of our planet or, alternatively, could be content to be judgmental or dismissive in their attitude toward them.

It is difficult to imagine the situation faced by Vasco da Gama when he landed in western India at the end of the fifteenth century and, seeing an image of a goddess in a Hindu temple, supposed it to be connected with a somewhat unusual cult of the Virgin Mary. How could he have understood this experience otherwise, coming as he did from a Christian Europe that had been virtually cut off from contact with India or the East? It is equally hard to think ourselves back into the mind of Thomas Colebrooke, a lawyer, who went to India in the eighteenth century to attempt to understand the Indian legal system. His mundane aim was to further his own career in the East India Company. In so doing he discovered that the Sanskrit word *dharma* meaning 'law' had religious as well as legal implications and, on the basis of this deeper understanding, he became the first westerner to summarise the six philosophical branches of the Hindu religious tradition. To us it may seem commonplace to stress the religious underpinnings of the Sanskrit language and the importance of philosophy within Indian religious culture; to Colebrooke, Sanskrit was an unknown language and Indian religion an unexplored area.[1]

Today, we know a lot about Indian religion and the other world religions. We have at our disposal an increasingly sophisticated awareness of the various religious traditions of the world, and we share an increasing conviction that Christian theology must grapple more deeply with the challenge and opportunity presented not only by the ever-growing data of world religions but also by the living world-views of other men and women in our world.

Indeed a main problem is the sheer vastness and diversity of our knowledge of both world religions and Christian theology.[2] The religious traditions of the world are many and complex and often differ as much (if not more) among themselves than by comparison with the Christian tradition. As we shall see, Christian theology itself is in disarray. There are diverse views as to the nature and purpose of Christian theology; there is a bewildering pluralism within contemporary Christian theology; there is no agreed expectation as to the results to be expected from Christian theological interpretations of other religions, either for Christian theology itself or for the religions concerned. The temptation is to throw up our hands in despair at the seeming impossibility of grappling efficiently with this topic.

At the level of contemporary global concern, which is becoming increasingly important for ordinary people and political leaders around the world, the issues are even deeper and more complex—and they have implications for the study and practice of Christian theology and world religions. The events surrounding the rise to power of the Ayatollah Khomeini in Iran have reminded us of the close relationship that exists between religious and other matters within another major religious tradition. The fact that the present Pope was born in Poland has wider than religious implications. The coming together, in the case of Israel, of two sensibilities, on the one hand the Jewish reaction to the horrors of the Holocaust and her sense that the setting up of the state of Israel is related to the Messianic vision and on the other hand the Muslim reaction to her former weakness at the hands of the 'Christian' West and her sense that Jerusalem is also an Islamic holy city, gives a religious dimension to the Middle Eastern situation which is clearly a global concern.

Quite apart from the examples just mentioned, there is a sense in which Christian theology and the study of world religions have an implicit concern in the general global issues of the planet earth. Although this implicit concern is not our sole interest in this book, it is instructive to pause for a moment and review these basic global issues which comprise, as it were, the scenario against the backdrop of which religious and other studies must increasingly be pursued.

At one level global problems seem to centre upon ecological and physical matters: the vanishing of various natural species of wild life due partly to the depradations of man, the pollution of parts of the global environment due to urbanisation and the like, the increasing search for energy at a world level, the diminishment of non-renewable mineral, oil and other planetary natural resources, and the increasing contamination of the atmosphere and biosphere through nuclear experiments and so forth. At a second level come more obviously human and social matters: the increasing poverty gap between rich and poor nations, the mounting figures of world population, the growing doubt as to whether world food supplies can keep pace with the mounting population spiral, the sexual revolution, the refugee problem, racial discrimination, the economic debate between the North and the South, the political debate between the East and the West, and (importantly) increasing nuclear proliferation and tensions. At a third level come more obviously moral and spiritual matters[3]: the moral and spiritual implications of the global use of space and the sea which belong in general to no particular nation, the moral and spiritual implications of the global use of genetics and electronics which potentially affect all humans, the perennial search for meaning that is common to humankind, and the suspicion that there appears to be arising a spiritual malaise, at any rate in the western part of the globe. There may be discussion as to whether, in this categorisation, the correct global issues are placed at the correct levels, there may even be discussion as to the correct designation of the levels themselves. What is less amenable to debate is the fact that these issues are real problems, and that they are problems of global import. It is also clear that Christian theology and the study of world religions have an overlapping interest in many or most of these concerns. Consequently, although many of these matters will not emerge directly within the pages of this book, they represent the implicit background against which our discussion will take place. After all, the religious traditions of the world are global in extent and any discussion of Christian theology and world religions must proceed within the wider framework of general global issues. We shall find, as we impinge upon these issues, that they not only influence but are also influenced by our more specific discussion.

However, while not denying the importance for our theme of the global context, our particular problem is how to limit our discussion in order to make it manageable and in order to cover the ground mapped out within the parameters of Christian theology and world religions. During the remainder of this opening chapter we will indicate how we intend to achieve this aim.

It is important to be clear at the outset that this book is primarily an exercise in Christian theology. Some, if not most, of the author's work has been conducted within the academic circle relating to world religions, and a feature of the theological exercise that forms the heart of this book will be a number of informed discussions of various aspects of world religions. However this volume is not an investigation of Comparative Religion as such. It is a study of Christian theology in its relationships with other religions. The scope of the discussion of other religions will be comprehensive, the treatment of other religions will be serious. There will even be, at points in the presentation, attempts to offer original insights into the study of world religions. Nevertheless such portraits of world religions, as and when they occur, will be part of a wider canvas centering upon Christian theology. As the title of the series suggests, the context of this work is *Contemporary Christian Studies*.

It is a noteworthy fact that relatively few Christian theologians have taken a deep interest in non-western religions. As Peter Berger puts it[4]:

Most Christian theology today, be it Protestant or Catholic, liberal or conservative, goes on as if the Judaeo-Christian tradition were alone in the world—with modern secularity as its only external conversation partner.

Things are beginning to change. A number of contemporary theologians are seeing the necessity for paying closer attention to the world-views of others. In 1981 David Tracy of Chicago wrote[5]:

A religion like Christianity, a religion which includes as its paradigmatic focal meaning the always-already, not-yet event of the grace of Jesus Christ, a religion which includes within itself the additional focal meanings of manifestation, proclamation and prophetic action, should be willing to enter into the conversation among the religions which the emerging future of a global humanity demands.

Elsewhere Brian Hebblethwaite comments[6]:

The relation between Christianity and other religions has become one of the most pressing themes for Christian self-understanding today.

These are straws in the wind that indicate an increasing awareness among Christian theologians that the great world religions are more than optional extras in any present-day study of Christian theology.

It will be the contention of this present work that the growing interest of Christian theologians and Christians generally in world religions must accelerate to a much deeper level of seriousness. Such an interest is not an optional extra, it is a necessity. Without it, Christians are unequipped for living in a global world. The great world religions do not merely offer *another* conversation partner to Christian theology along with modern secularity, they are at least equal in importance as conversation partners. It is not only the relation between Christianity and other religions that is pressing but also how Christianity can learn from other religions. It is relevant to ask what the Christian approach should be to other world religions, and it is just as important to determine how the Christian tradition can further evolve and renew itself by means of its contact with those religions. Our theme is not secondary, it is primary. It finds its level of importance not on the circumference of the theological circle but near the centre of that circle. Our theme is so important that in a small book such as this there will be space to do little more than to evoke a consciousness of its cruciality, to indicate the main directions for its further exploration, and to inspire, perhaps even jolt, the reader into his or her own wrestling with its implications for the Christian person, Christian theology, and the world in general.

Like a piece of music, our work is based upon a main theme, Christian theology and world religions, but contained within it are nine variations which in their interplay interpret and expand the dominant harmony. Some of these variations are covered explicitly in particular chapters, others are integrated more subtly into the total body of the work. We will summarise them briefly now as a way of anticipating the basic issues that will be raised in the discussion that is to follow.

(i) How can we understand world religions without distorting or judging them? This is a problem for scholars of religion as well as for theologians, but it is especially pressing for theologians. The number of Christian theologians who have brought a deep knowledge, understanding and empathy to their comments on other religions can be counted on the fingers of two hands. Honourable mention may certainly be given to Rudolf Otto, Nathan Söderblom, and Paul Tillich who toward the end of his life was becoming fascinated by the prospects opened up for Christian theology by a study of other religions, especially Buddhism[7]. In Britain, theologians such as John Hick, and in the United States theologians such as John Cobb, George Rupp, Gordon Kaufman, David Tracy, and Langdon Gilkey, and on the continent of Europe theologians such as Wolfhart Pannenberg and Heinrich Dumoulin have begun to grapple with the issues concerned[8]. Too often, however, western Christian theologians have offered opinions about other religions from a basis of ignorance, or have interpreted them (and therefore misinterpreted them) in the light of Christian theology. Other religions were seen not in their own light, nor according to the informed viewpoints of adherents of those religions, but through the pre-focused lenses of Christian theology.

There is the old Irish joke, 'If I wanted to get to Dublin,

I wouldn't start from here'. The Christian theologian may be tempted to say, if I want to understand the Hindu tradition I wouldn't start from Christian theology. As we shall see, there may well be some truth in this. However, if the Christian theologian is to remain such rather than becoming an historian of religion he will sooner or later have to relate his understanding of other religions to Christian theology. The problem nevertheless remains, how can the Christian theologian understand and empathise with other religions without distorting or judging them, and how can he at the same time remain a Christian theologian?

In this book we will offer three suggestions to enable the Christian to understand and empathise with other religions. There is pre-supposed, of course, the willingness to do some study of another religion (or other religions), if possible to talk to participants in other religions, and if the opportunity arises, to visit the core areas of other religions.

In the first place, we offer a model for the understanding of any religious tradition, including Christianity. According to this model, each major religion has lying behind it a notion of (indeed a reality of) transcendence, and each tradition points to a mediating focus whereby transcendent reality is made meaningful to people on earth (for Christians it would be God mediated through Christ). The model then points to eight observable elements that are present within every religious tradition:– a religious community (in Christianity the church), ritual (sacraments, festivals, liturgies), social involvement (relationships with wider society), ethics (precepts and practices for the good life), scripture and myth (the Bible and its tales), concepts (doctrines that are philosophically supported), aesthetics (religious music, painting, sculpture, buildings, iconography, literature), and spirituality (prayers, etc.). Underlying these elements and giving them life is the religious intention, perhaps we can even say the 'faith', of the people concerned. We shall contend that this model, which will be expanded later, can make sense of the major religious traditions: the Christian, Jewish, Muslim, Hindu, and Buddhist. It is helpful and comforting to the Christian theologian to have a framework of such 'elements' whereby he or she can understand analogically the data of other religions, although we shall also contend that this 'grid' brings out the differences as well as the similarities between religions.

In the second place, we offer a historical model of the history of world religions from early man to the present day. It is only in our own day that such a unified historical model has become possible. We have become used to thinking in terms of the history of separate religions (Christianity, Judaism, Islam, Hinduism, Buddhism, etc.), and separate cultures and civilisations (Europe, the Middle East, India, China, etc.) as though they were distinct entities. There are complex reasons for the rise of this sort of thinking in the past, and there are equally complex reasons for the passing of this sort of thinking in the present. We are content, in this introduction, to allude to one such reason, namely the emergence of a global consciousness in response to the global problems we outlined earlier. To this breakthrough to global consciousness, each religion, culture and civilisation brings its own history, but no longer in isolation. There is the exciting and perhaps disturbing awareness that no religion or civilisation is 'in it alone'. We share a converging past and a related future. Our second model will enable the Christian theologian to see other religions not only as traditions containing eight integrated elements by means of which faithful people appropriate mediated transcendent reality but also as dynamic, evolving traditions that are part of a converging historical process. In other words, Judaism, Islam, Hinduism and Buddhism are not really static 'isms', like Christianity they are moving traditions[9]. They bring their own treasures (and failures) to the collective global consciousness of the future, and the same prophetic urgency that enables us to prepare for that global future enables us also to see the apparently separate histories of the past as part of the same continuum.

In the third place, we will suggest the value of the Christian, after having understood the basic elements and the historical flow of another tradition, 'passing over' into it through the creative use of imagination[10]. Realising, through this imaginative leap, what it means for a Hindu to be a Hindu and a Muslim to be a Muslim, the Christian can then return to his or her own tradition and theological roots and renew them through the creative experience that has been undergone.

(ii) In our first variation on the general theme of Christian theology and world religions, we have suggested a threefold reconnaissance method of approaching and grasping the significance of other religions. Let it not be thought that by means of this or any other approach we will fully understand any other religious tradition, not to mention other religions in general. It will hopefully make it possible for us to understand *something* about those of another religion although it is inconceivable that this or any other imaginative stratagem would lead us to understand *everything* about those of another religion.

Indeed our second variation raises the whole question of what we mean by Christian theology. To be sure, Christian theology is not a monolithic corpus, awesome in its majestic unity, that stands solid and foursquare in face of the disordered and jumbled patterns by means of which we attempt to understand the intricacies of the other world religions. As George Rupp points out, Christian theology mirrors within itself the pluralism of world religions.[11] Contemporary Christian theology is chaotically plural. Not to mention the variations between the theologies of different churches (Roman Catholic, Orthodox, Baptist, Pentecostal, etc.), Christian theologians have engaged in biblical criticism, they have demythologised with Bultmann, they have adapted neo-orthodoxies arising out of Barth, they have responded to A. J. Ayer's *Language, Truth and Logic* through the defence of 'God-talk', they have wondered whether God was dead, they have experimented with process thought, they have tried the theological path of creative evolution, they have discussed the sociological role of the minister or the church, they have reinterpreted credal beliefs, they have rethought the meaning of liturgy, they have explored situational ethics, they have discussed liberation theology, black theology, feminine theology (and other theologies we have no time to mention here)[12]. It is not too much to claim that Christian theology is in disarray. Before Christian theology can meaningfully consider its approach to world religions, or consider how it can renew itself through its contact with world religions, there is the need for Christian theologians to be clearer about what Christian theology basically is. In this book, we will examine the history of the word 'theology' from Greek times through the history of the church in order to discover what 'theology' has meant for Christians until now. Without pre-empting our discoveries in full, we are content to intimate three ways in which our research accords with the models set out in variation number one. It appears that theology has to do with God, with knowledge of God, with transcendence; theology develops within a historical tradition that is in dynamic process so that theology is continually developing both by reflection upon and interpretation of the past and by new contacts in the present; and theology, although not remote from any of the eight elements outlined in our first mode, has to do especially with *concepts* and *spirituality*. In other words, our attempt to understand what another religion is can help us in our search to understand what Christian theology is. The two are not unrelated.

(iii) Throughout virtually the whole history of the Christian church, theology has been equated with Christian theology. By investigating the meaning of the word 'theology' back into Graeco-Roman times, there emerges the interesting point that at that period, and again in our own time, the notion of 'theology' need not necessarily be allied to a particular religious community. For the Greeks and Romans, theology could be conceived as being part of a general education. It was a subject of study, at first bound up with the early Greek myths concerning the gods, later associated also with the study of philosophy wherein God could be conceived as 'World Reason', the 'Divine', or 'Being'. In neither case was membership of a religious community necessary to the study of 'theology'. The same tendency to distance the study of theology from membership of a religious community is observable today in parts of

the West, and especially in the United States. For example
Gordon Kaufman writes[13] about:

> an understanding of theology as not primarily a parochial
> or churchly activity but a public discipline dealing with
> the inescapable human problem of orientation in life and
> in the world.

This sort of statement points to an implied difference
between 'Christian theology' as the conceptual and experiential agonising of the Christian community and 'theology'
as a humane educational activity. In the case of Kaufman
and those like him there is the further complication that
their notion of 'theology', although distanced from the
Christian community, retains a Christian flavour.

The discourse in this present book (although relating to
both) relates more to Christian theology than to theology,
and that for two main reasons. Our concern is for Christian
theology throughout time and throughout space. It is fair
to say that most of the present discussion of theology as a
general educational discipline has emerged in the West,
and that much of it is a product of Protestant thinking. To
that extent it is parochial rather than being representative.
Moreover insofar as this discussion has to do genuinely
with 'theology' as a secular discipline rather than 'Christian
theology' its potential usefulness lies outside the Christian
tradition in the cognitive realm of education and the
humanities as academic fields.

(iv) In recent times one or two influential scholars have
pointed out a third possible meaning of the word theology
that is more closely related to our topic of Christian
theology and world religions. Wilfred Cantwell Smith has
pleaded for earnest thought concerning the setting up of a
theology of comparative religion. His search is for universal
theological categories that will be theologically viable not
only for Christianity but also for the other religions of the
world. He calls for a global theology of religion that will
do justice to 'the emergence of a global and verified self-
consciousness of religious diversity',[14] and a 'theology of

religions' that will be 'the product of thinkers who see, who feel, and indeed, who know, men and women of all religious groups and all centuries, as members of one community, one in which they themselves participate'[15]. Unlike Kaufman and his colleagues, who are taking theology away from its connection with the Christian tradition into wider secular society, Smith is expanding Christian theology into the wider area of world religions. As he puts it, 'Without being a Christian theology it would be invalid if it were not Christian'[16]. Later in this book we will have cause to spend some time upon a critique of this intriguing thesis. Another Smith, Huston Smith, offers a variation upon this theme of Cantwell Smith's that is at the same time both close to it and distant from it. According to Huston Smith and a group of scholars who espouse what they term the 'perennial philosophy', there is underlying the religious traditions of the world a perennial philosophy or a perennial theology that provides a basic unity for religions that are outwardly very different. The perennial theology or philosophy that Huston Smith alludes to is, like Wilfred Cantwell Smith's theology of religion, Christian yet more than Christian; however it is not, as in Wilfred Smith's case, a sheaf of universal theological categories applicable conceptually to all the world religions: it is the 'primordial tradition', the 'forgotten truth' lying behind them all[17]. In due course, we will comment further upon the similarities and differences between the views of the two Smiths and we will intimate why neither, although interesting and significant, coincide with the notion of Christian theology in its relation to world religions that is held in this book.

(v) A fifth variation, prompted directly by the fourth, plays upon the distinction between the study of Christian theology and the study of world religions. There are subtle and important differences between the two enterprises and it is crucial that these differences should be recognised. This discussion as to the boundary lines to be drawn up between the two fields of study will underly much of what we have to say. For example, we will attempt to show that Wilfred Cantwell Smith's work lies primarily in the field of comparative religion and history of religions rather than in theology however defined. Nevertheless there is a close relationship between Christian theology and world religions as fields of study. To distinguish between them is not to deny the close interaction that can exist between the two areas. To clarify the distinction is to allow the possibility of closer ties developing.

(vi) An important aspect of much earlier study of the relationship between Christian theology and world religions was an analysis of the attitude that Christian theology ought to take towards world religions. This question remains relevant. At the appropriate point, we will analyse the seven main theological attitudes that Christian theologians have taken towards world religions. We will not make value judgments in relation to these seven stances. We will summarise them dispassionately. They operate on a spectrum that ranges from exclusivism at the one extreme to relativism on the other. Clearly the type of theological attitude that is taken bears some relationship to the view of Christian theology that is held and the amount and quality of knowledge there is concerning world religions. Therefore tunes from other variations mingle with and inform this one.

(vii) It is not enough to ask the question, what are the theological attitudes that Christians should take towards other traditions? More important is to grapple with the question of how Christian theology can renew itself and further evolve by contact with and response to the world's religions. Throughout its history, Christian theology has developed by internal reflection and external encounter, and by internal reflection *upon* external encounter. There has been a continual process of interaction between the Christian tradition and the context in which it found itself. This process began early on when the disciples of Jesus, who were Jews with a Hebrew outlook, saw the Christian community expand into the Gentile world which operated with a different world-view. St Paul exhibited in his own person three aspects of his own world—he was a Hebrew of the Hebrews, a Roman citizen, and steeped in Greek culture. James Dunn has shown how the early church was not monolithic. It contained four strands; the Hebrew Christians, the apocalyptic Christians, the Johannine Christians, and the Pauline Christians.[18] Although the early Christians inherited a mainly Hebrew view of God, the New Testament spoke of *theos* rather than *'el, 'eloah*, or *'elohim*, and the word *theologia* itself is a Greek word. Christian theology thus came to be couched in Greek terms, and Jaeger has shown how the thought of Origen, Clement of Alexandria, the Cappadocian Fathers and other Christian thinkers of the early period was influenced not only by the terminology but also by the content of Greek thought[19]. Meanwhile, in the Latin West, Christian theology as exemplified in men such as Tertullian and St Augustine became couched in Latin terminology and it inherited Roman modes of thought. If we may suppose for a moment that the early Christian community had, for historical reasons, expanded east into Persia or India rather than predominantly west into the Mediterranean world, it can hardly be doubted that Christian theology would have developed along somewhat different lines and that the history of the Christian tradition would have been different. As it was, the Christian destiny lay mainly in Europe, and Christian theology developed in Europe at a time when Europe was largely cut off from the rest of the world. Successive waves of barbarian invaders, ranging from the Goths to the Vikings, were incorporated into the developing Christian tradition, and they made an important contribution to the further development of that tradition, influenced as they were by centres so disparate as Celtic Ireland in the West, Rome in the South, and Byzantium to the East. However, the Christian theological dialogue was perforce mainly internal. The eastern religions were virtually unknown. Islam and Judaism were misunderstood or viewed as heretical forms of Christianity. Even the incorporation into Christian theology by Aquinas of the newly discovered thought of Aristotle, creative as his magnificent synthesis was, heralded merely the successful encounter of Christian theology with another *western* mode of thought.

The contemporary situation is genetically different from

the earlier one, which constituted a 'European captivity of the church'[20], in two ways. Firstly we now live, as has been stressed before, in a global world. Forces accumulating in the West, influenced partly by elements within the Judaeo-Christian world-view, have built up for many generations to unify the human race within a single web of interlinked communications. The scientific, industrial and technological revolutions have conspired, in an accelerating degree, to produce a global community that can view itself as one from space—a global community that transcends the former boundaries of religion and culture. This globalising process, as we have already shown, has created global problems; moreover, although the roots of this process may have arisen within the Judaeo-Christian tradition, they have now spread beyond it. A lot of the time and energy of contemporary Christian theology is taken up by the dialogue with various types of global technology and modernity.

Secondly the very fact of globalisation has opened up exciting new possibilities of growth for Christian theology. She is now exposed to contact with the world-views of the major religions that were formerly unknown. The Christian tradition is thrown into dialogue with the other religious traditions for the fashioning of a new global community. Christian theology is granted new partners in conversation, new touchstones for her own renewal. There is the possibility for the reclaiming of insights that lie dormant within the universal Christian tradition and which can be re-enlivened by sparks from without. Other religions provide dynamically new possibilities for the reshaping of Christian theology in a number of ways. It is part of the purpose of this book to make this point forcibly.

(viii) In some ways, it would appear that the enlivening contact of Christian theology with world religions, together with the growth of indigenous Christian theologies that is linked with the wider development, only serves to deepen the theological cacophony that has previously been alluded to. If to all the other theological movements that have been spawned in recent times we have to add indigenous Indian,

African, Japanese, Chinese and other Christian theologies, does not this merely aggravate the situation? Clearly in some ways it does. However we also wish to suggest that the encouragement given to Christian theology by its contact with world religions to clarify its views as to its own nature, to think in terms of Christianity as a comprehensive ongoing tradition, and to renew itself globally—all this raises the important question as to whether we can take an overview of the seemingly chaotic theological situation and begin to think again in terms of some sort of emerging systematic theology. Clearly this is a transitional and plural stage for Christian theology. It is our contention that the Christian theological debate with world religions may not only complicate the possibility of an emergent systematic theology but also paradoxically increase the chances of this happening.

(ix) Our final variation will involve the application of some of the ideas we have introduced in this work to a specific symbol within Christian theology, namely the Trinity. How can we achieve a wider and deeper view of the Trinity through the mediating photographic negative of world religions? How can we begin to think in terms of an emerging systematic theology as we look at the specific symbol of the Trinity? The example we have chosen is not arbitrary. It represents the Christian view of God and transcendence, and the Christian mediating focus. We have suggested that the reality of transcendence and a mediating focus are the keys to our model for the understanding of any religious tradition. We have also intimated that the notion of God is one of the keys to any understanding of theology. It is therefore fitting that the Trinity should provide the example for the outworking of our theological ideas.

The aim of this series, *Contemporary Christian Studies*, is to promote thought among Christians about the contemporary world, and about how Christians should approach that world theologically. The aim of this present volume, *Christian Theology and World Religions—A Global Approach*, is to stimulate reflection about a whole range of issues concerning Christian theology and world religions. We have purposely introduced all the main questions related to this topic, because there is no other book that has dealt with them all, and we feel that it is vital that Christian theology should take an overview of the entire field. In addition to opening up for the reader the whole gamut of topics relating to Christian theology and world religions, we have indicated what appears to us to be the appropriate path for Christian theology to take. It is our conviction that this whole area of the Christian encounter with and response to world religions is probably the most important question facing Christian theology today. In studying this book the reader will be given methods of understanding world religions and Christian theology, and a stimulus to search for a new understanding of our global situation.

This book could easily have been twice or three times its present length. Nevertheless in spite of the constraints placed upon book length by the series, perhaps even because of the clarity and brevity imposed by page numbers, it is likely that when the reader puts this book down his or her theological thinking will never be quite the same again.

FOOTNOTES

1. See John Keay, *India Discovered*, Windward, Leicester, 1981; P J Marshall, (ed), *The British Discovery of Hinduism*, Cambridge University Press, 1970.

2. For content of world religions see Charles J. Adams, (ed), *A Reader's Guide to the Great Religions*, The Free Press, New York, 1977; for method see Frank Whaling, (ed), *Contemporary Approaches to the Study of Religion*, vol 1, *The Humanities* & vol 2, *The Social Sciences*, Mouton, Berlin New York Amsterdam, 1984, 1985.

3. See Ervin Laszlo *et al*, *Goals for Mankind: A Report to the Club of Rome on the New Horizons of the Global Community*, Dutton, New York, 1977.

4. Peter Berger, *The Heretical Imperative*, Collins, London, 1980, p 166.

5. David Tracy, *The Analogical Imagination*, Crossroad, New York, 1981, p 450.

6. John Hick & Brian Hebblethwaite, (eds), *Christianity and Other Religions*, Collins, London, 1980, p 7

7. See J Waardenburg, *Classical Approaches to the Study of Religion*, vol 2, Mouton, The Hague, 1974, on Otto (pp 200–6) and Söderblom

(pp 266–72); and P Tillich, 'The Significance of the History of Religions for the Systematic Theologian' in Jerald Brauer, (ed), *The Future of Religions*, Harper and Row, New York, 1966.

8. See John Hick, *God and the Universe of Faiths*, Macmillan, London, 1973; John Cobb, *Christ in a Pluralistic Culture*, Westminster, Philadelphia, 1975; George Rupp, *Christologies and Cultures*, Mouton, The Hague, 1974; Gordon Kaufman, *The Theological Imagination*, Westminster, Philadelphia, 1981; David Tracy, *The Analogical Imagination*, Crossroad, New York, 1981; Langdon Gilkey, *Reaping the Whirlwind*, Seabury, New York, 1976; Wolfhart Pannenberg, *Theology and the Philosophy of Science*, Westminster, Philadelphia, 1976; Heinrich Dumoulin, *Christianity Meets Buddhism*, Open Court, La Salle, 1974.

9. The classical statement on 'isms' and reification is in Wilfred Cantwell Smith, *The Meaning and End of Religion*, New American Library, New York, 1966.

10. See John S Dunne, *The Way of all the Earth*, Notre Dame, Indiana, 1978.

11. George Rupp, *Beyond Existentialism and Zen*, Oxford University Press, New York, 1979, pp 9–16.

12. See J Macquarrie, *The Scope of Demythologising: Bultmann and his Critics*, Harper, New York, 1961, R Bultmann, *Faith and Understanding*, SCM Press, London, 1969; John Bowden, *Karl Barth*, SCM Press, London, 1971, K Barth, *Dogmatics in Outline*, SCM Press, London, 1949; A J Ayer, *Language, Truth and Logic*, Gollancz, London, 1946, J Macquarrie, *God-Talk*, SCM Press, London, 1967; T J J Altizer, *The Gospel of Christian Atheism*, Collins, London, 1967; C Hartshorne, *The Divine Relativity*, Yale University Press, Newhaven, 1948, Schubert M. Ogden, *The Reality of God*, Harper & Row, New York, 1966; Teilhard de Chardin, *l'Avenir de l'Homme*, Editions du Seuil, Paris, 1959; M Hill, *A Sociology of Religion*, Heinneman, London, 1973; J Hick, *The Myth of God Incarnate*, SCM Press, London 1977; E Schillebeeckx, *The Eucharist*, Sheed & Ward, London, 1968; J Fletcher, *Situation Ethics*, Westminster, Philadelphia, n.d.; G Gutierrez, *A Theology of Liberation*, SCM Press, London, 1974; J H Cone, *Black Theology and Black Power*, Seabury, New York, 1969; Mary Daly, *Beyond God the Father*, Beacon Paperback, Boston, 1974.

13. This is the burden of the book by G Kaufman, *The Theological Imagination*, Westminster, Philadelphia, 1981.

14. Wilfred Cantwell Smith, *Towards a World Theology*, Westminster Press, Philadelphia, 1981, p 124.

15. *Ibid*, p 125.

16. *Ibid*, p 125.

17. Huston Smith, *Forgotten Truth: The Primordial Tradition*, Harper & Row, New York, 1976.

18. James D. G. Dunn, *Unity and Diversity in the New Testament*, SCM Press, London, 1977.

19. Werner Jaeger, *Early Christianity and Greek Paideia*, Belknap Press for Harvard University Press, Cambridge, 1962.

20. As R H S Boyd has shown in *An Introduction to Indian Christian Theology*, CLS, Madras, 1969.

CHAPTER TWO

UNDERSTANDING WORLD RELIGIONS

When confronted with the bewildering array of the world's religious traditions many people, both participants and onlookers, are beset by an incipient failure of nerve. One's initial tendency in face of the vast amount of data that flicker over the screen of the mind like successive images in a game of space invaders is to succumb to a mental paralysis that inhibits the desire to make sense of the whole.

The reflective person who wishes to construct an order of understanding out of the apparent chaos is faced by problems. The theologian may see the need to grapple with the field of world religions but is inhibited by the further work involved in achieving an adequate insight into this area of knowledge. The historian of religion, who may have deep expertise in one language or group of languages (Sanskrit, Arabic, Pali, Chinese, Hebrew, Greek) or one particular religion or area (Hinduism, Islam, Buddhism, Judaism, Christianity, Indology, Sinology, the Middle East), is tempted to take refuge in his or her own speciality and profess incompetence to survey the vast panorama of the totality of world religions. The cry goes up, 'it is outside my field'.

The sheer volume of information about world religions is a problem in itself. As Louis Henry Jordan put it in 1905:

'The accumulation of information, indeed, has never slackened for a moment; and the special embarrassment of today is the overwhelming mass of detail, still rapidly increasing, which confronts every earnest investigator.'[1]

If this statement was apposite in 1905, it is even more true in our own age when quicker communications in both transport and electronics deluge us with an ever-increasing mass of data. To be sure this kind of comment would apply equally to *all* areas of knowledge in our 'age of specialisation', but this does not lessen its validity in regard to world religions.

It is the aim of this chapter to post some guidelines by means of which a newcomer to the scene may gain an immediate access to a framework of understanding of world religions. Indeed, by means of the pegs that will shortly be marked out, it is hoped that theologians and students of religion who already have some facility in analysis may be helped to a deeper awareness of the facts and issues concerned. The schemes of interpretation that follow are based upon a distillation of the author's work in other fields and will be of especial interest to contemporary Christians attempting to reflect creatively upon the present and past world religious scene.

I. A HISTORICAL INTERPRETATION OF HUMAN RELIGIOUSNESS

(a) Introduction. It is impossible to do more in one short chapter than sketch in refined shorthand a map of the global history of religion.

To summarise the problem, how can we comprehend in a single historical continuum the separate histories of the major traditions: Christianity, Judaism, Islam, Hinduism and Buddhism? How can we also include some treatment of religious traditions that have died out or had less influence? What, for example, of Palaeolithic and Neolithic religion; Mesopotamian and Egyptian religion; Steppe Shamanism and Canaanite religion; Greek, Roman, Gnostic and Manichaean religion; Confucian, Taoist and Shinto religion in China and Japan; the Jains in India and Zoroaster in Iran; the Aztecs, Incas and Mayas of the Americas; the Sikhs; the primal religions of Africa, Australasia and America; and the many new religions of the modern world? In what way is it possible to include within the same conceptual picture the non-violence of the Jain monk and the bloodthirsty sacrifices of the Aztecs, the virtual absence of gods in ancient China and the plurality of gods in the Hindu pantheon, the insistence upon One God of prophetic religion and the denial of

God by the quasi-religion we call communism, the suffering of Christ upon the cross and the serenity of the Buddha's enlightenment? A mere statement of the questions highlights the dilemma.

We have stated in no uncertain terms the nature of the problem by which we are confronted, and before we feel overwhelmed by it let us summarise the nature of the reinterpretation of the history of religion that we offer in this chapter.

(b) Palaeolithic religion. It is difficult to estimate when humankind first appeared on earth. Hypothetically, this may have happened twenty million years ago. The first concrete evidence, discovered by Mary Leakey in 1976 (footprints found in volcanic ash at Laetoli in Tanzania), shows how 'hominids three-and-three-quarter million years ago walked upright with a free-striding gait, just as we do today'[2]. It is dangerous to generalise about humanity's early religiousness—artefacts and skeletons give unclear evidence. Suffice it to say that, although the Leakeys' evidence is inconclusive, Peking Man (dating back about half a million years) and other early skeletal finds show signs of ritual treatment of skulls; from the middle Palaeolithic period (75–50,000 BC) there is increasing evidence of burial; and from the later Palaeolithic period (30,000 BC onwards) there is the evidence of cave art and all these have religious overtones[3].

Anthropologists tend to suggest that there is an element of continuity between early humanity and present-day tribal peoples. Insofar as this is the case (and it is debateable) it is clear that primal humanity did not invent the gods. They were contemporary with the rise of human conscious awareness. In human consciousness the gods pre-existed humankind, so that awareness of nature, awareness of humanity, and awareness of the gods were all part of primal humanity's consciousness. To that extent, religiousness was part of primal humanity's being, part of what made humanity human.

Whether primal humanity's awareness was of the gods, God, or both is a moot point of academic discussion. For Darwin and the early anthropologists it was of the gods. As Darwin puts it, in the *Descent of Man*:

'If, however, we include under the term religion the belief in unseen spiritual agencies, the case is wholly different, for this belief seems to be universal with the less civilised races.'[4]

Later scholars, such as Lang and Schmidt, were not so sure. Schmidt posited the theory of an original High God in the primal consciousness, and suggested that this original monotheism became modified later into a belief in the gods. More recent scholarship has pointed out that primal religion is a complex affair about which it is unwise to generalise, and that different primal tribes often have *both* the notion of a High God *and* the notion of intermediate gods. Talk of either monotheism or polytheism becomes inappropriate. Primal humanity's consciousness was (and is) peculiar to primal humanity; in it transcendence (whether in terms of God or the gods), humankind and nature were held together in primordial unity. Mircea Eliade tells us that part of our western problem is:

How to assimilate culturally the spiritual universes that Africa, Oceania, South-East Asia open to us?[5]

I would suggest, in the context of this book, that part of our Christian theological problem is how to assimilate theologically the spiritual universe opened up to us by primal humanity. For that spiritual universe has to do not only with primal humanity's consciousness but also with a primal part of our *own* consciousness.

(c) Neolithic religion. Our Palaeolithic ancestors succeeded in surviving in nature by chipping stone tools, inventing the bow, domesticating dogs, and using the power of painting. The Neolithic revolution (starting about 10,000 BC) gave human beings a closer relationship with nature and the beginnings of mastery over it by the invention of spinning, weaving, pottery, and (above all) agriculture and animal husbandry. Neolithic humanity's relationship with transcendence remained close as well, for the sacred was seen to be at work in the cyclical processes of nature as well as in humans. There

was an increasingly intimate relationship between human beings, the earth they were learning to harness, and the transcendent powers they felt to reside in both. Indeed, Christian theology has something to learn from the ecological feel for nature that is part of the culture of people such as the American Indians, for this is similar by analogy to the ecological 'feel' of Neolithic humankind.

(d) Rise of town civilisations in the early near east. The Palaeolithic revolution which saw the emergence of the human race as we know it into the light of history, and the Neolithic revolution centred upon the discovery of agriculture, remain the decisive breakthroughs in our planetary story beside which even our contemporary global achievements seem small. The rise of civilisation in a form more recognisable to modern persons dates back to the beginnings of town civilisations, first in Mesopotamia and then in Egypt around 3,500 BC. These were accompanied by the rise of similar civilisations in the Indus Valley of the Indian sub-continent (by diffusion) and in what is now China (by spontaneous creation). The invention of the plough, the use of irrigation, the development of sea travel, the emergence of metallurgy and the rise of writing enabled towns to develop in which agriculture was no longer the sole concern, and in which inter-connections with other areas became easier through transport, trade and literature. Religious factors were important in promoting this development. As McNeill puts it:

'For the first time in human history the Sumerian temple community technically permitted and psychologically compelled the production of an agricultural surplus and applied that surplus to support specialists, who became, as city dwellers have sinced remained, the creators, sustainers, and organisers of civilised life.'[6]

This period in the history of religion, which saw the emergence of separate priesthoods, temple buildings, great festivals, Sumerian and later theologies, and sacred kingship (symbolised in the Pharaoh of Egypt), does not merit elaborate mention in our narrative. Nevertheless it is important. Just as Palaeolithic religion reminds us that religiousness is part of humanity's basic inheritance, and Neolithic religion reminds us that humankind's concordat with nature is not broken with impunity, Mesopotamian religion reminds us that religion has had its part in creating as well as conserving civilisation. Indeed, as the Genesis myth of the Garden of Eden points out symbolically, creativity has disruptive as well as positive possibilities. In order for the human race to advance in knowledge and civilisation it had to fall from its original innocence of the unity of transcendence, humankind and nature. The fall was a *culpa* (fault) in that it broke this innocence; it was also a *felix culpa* (a happy fault) in that it enabled humans to advance in knowledge and civilisation. Nevertheless, the relationship between God, humanity and nature remained close. We see this in the shamanism of the Steppe peoples of Central Asia, and we see it in the myths of the barbarian invaders who erupted out of the Steppe to sow the seeds of future civilisations—the Aryans into India, the Hittites into the Middle East, the Mycenae into Europe, and the Shang into China. The odd men out in this story were the Jews who were a suffering as well as an invading people. By resisting the nature myths of those around them the Jews exalted the Lord who had created the earth, they exalted humanity which had dominion over the earth under God, they prefigured the glories of the Judaeo-Christian doctrines of God and personhood, and they anticipated too the deficiencies of the Judaeo–Christian doctrine of nature.

(e) The Axial Period to 16th century AD. The broad brush strokes we have painted of the early religious history of the human race proved to be a prelude to the religious breakthrough of what has become known as the Axial Period. This centred upon the sixth century BC, and this century and those immediately before and after provided a watershed in human development. This period was normative in the rise of four great civilisations, those of India, China, Europe, and the Middle East in its later phase. Central to the future development of these civilisations was the presence during this age of creative religious leaders in these four corners of the earth. In India during the sixth century BC, the Buddha and the

Jain Mahavira were alive and the great Hindu Upanishads appeared; in China, Confucius was alive and the early evidences of Taoist and other influential currents were emerging; further West the Ionian philosophers prefigured the glory that was to be Greece and later Europe; and in the Middle East of the sixth century BC, there lived some of the great Hebrew prophets of Israel, and there were also the outworkings of Zoroaster and his work in Persia[7].

This was a humanly and religiously outstanding period. It was a period in which religious factors were of primary importance not only because of the significance of the figures concerned but also because of the consequences of their work for future history. Indeed, as we look at the broad sweep of human history, we can see that from about the sixth century BC to the sixteenth century AD four separate areas arose in the world that were more or less equal, more or less parallel, and more or less isolated. They were Europe stemming from Greece (and partly from Israel) and leading on into Christian civilisation; the Middle East declining at first from its former greatness but passing, through mainly Jewish and Zoroastrian sources, into the later grandeur of Muslim civilisation; India building a multi-religious civilisation on the basis of Aryan and Dravidian (Hindu) sources but using also Buddhist, Jain and even Christian, Parsi and Muslim influences; and China resting its civilisation upon the Confucian synthesis of the Han dynasty (c 200 BC to 200 AD) to which was added the leavening influence of Mahayana Buddhism. Speaking in broad terms we may therefore say that during the two thousand year period from about 500 BC to 1500 AD there were four great civilisations (with their cultural offshoots) in the four main centres of the world at the heart of which were the four great religious traditions of Christianity, Islam, Hinduism and Buddhism. The Jews remained the exception in that they remained a great religious tradition by contrast with the Mesopotamian, Egyptian, Graeco-Roman, and Gnostic religions which died out, and yet they were not at the centre of any great civilisation.

(i) As we look back upon the two thousand year period from about 500 BC to 1500 AD, we have space for brief comment on five matters. In the first place, as we have pointed out, there was an intimate connection between religious and general history in the four Euro-Asian areas we have highlighted. European civilisation became Christian civilisation, Middle Eastern civilisation became Muslim civilisation, Indian civilisation became largely Hindu civilisation, and Chinese civilisation was founded upon the Confucian, Taoist and Mahayana Buddhist traditions. To attempt to understand the Europe, Middle East, India, and China of the period we are discussing without stressing Christianity, Islam, Indian religion and Chinese religion would be rather like attempting to understand Hamlet by stressing the supporting characters rather than the Prince of Denmark himself. In other words, in evolving themselves, the great religious traditions were also creating great civilisations superior in scope and achievement to those that had gone before.

(ii) Part of the reason for this general religious impact upon cultures was the development in depth and intensity of the religions concerned. Paradoxically an element in this depth and intensity was the fact that the great religious traditions were *not* completely bound up in the civilisations that they formed. Their ultimate aims and motivations transcended their cultures in a way that had not been true of earlier or primal religions. Their final goal lay beyond this world in heaven and hell, or in release from the round of rebirths; their transcendent reference, whether it be God, Allah, Yahweh, Brahman, or Nirvana, was not circumscribed by earthly limits; their key symbol, whether it be Christ, the Koran, the Torah, the Atman, or the Dharma, was transmundane. Moreover their religious community was not absolutely equivalent to the general community; their worship although widespread was not usually obligatory; their ethics and their social involvement were often exemplary rather than traditional; their scriptures and concepts set standards to be achieved rather than realities already gained; and their insights into aesthetic beauty and spirituality indicated a vision desired rather than a world obtained.

Indeed, so deep and intense were the religions concerned that we can discern the coming to fruition, during this period, of religious seeds sown during the Axial Age. Christ was born at a time when the European and Middle Eastern worlds were open due in part to the journeys of Alexander the Great who crossed a kind of invisible barrier that even then separated West from East; and Christ was interpreted in the light of the Axial insights of Hebrew prophecy and Greek thought. The rise of Islam, although triggered by the religious genius of Muhammad, and influenced partly by Christian notions, heralded a creative reinterpretation of the Hebrew and Zoroastrian prophetic world view of the Axial Age; it signalled, as it were, the re-emergence of a strong Middle Eastern civilisation more dependent upon prophetic monotheism than Greek philosophy and Roman law. In India the master conceptions of the Upanishads—Brahman as Ultimate Reality, the Atman as the Inner Self of man, the essential oneness of Brahman and the Self, salvation as the realisation of this oneness, the human problem as an inability to achieve this realisation without inward knowledge, and the human plight as continual rebirth according to our deeds until this release through realisation is achieved—were interpreted and responded to in a multitude of different ways in the development of what we now term the Hindu tradition. The Buddha, who also lived in the India of the sixth century BC, was interpreted and responded to in vastly different ways, first in India and South East Asia, later in China and the Far East. In this way what we now call the Buddhist tradition was built up. The intermingling of this tradition with Confucian and Taoist elements in China and Confucian, Taoist and Shinto elements in Japan helped to create Chinese and Japanese civilisation.

(iii) In the third place, the sheer creativity of the religions we have mentioned led to their different evolution within their separate civilisations. Conversely the relative lack of creativity within other religions of the time, for example Graeco–Roman religion, Mesopotamian and Egyptian religion, the mystery religions, Zoroastrianism, the Jains,

and Christian groups outside Europe, resulted in their disappearance or lack of growth. Although we have stressed the Axial Age of the sixth century BC, it would be wrong to overstress it. Not only were Christ, Muhammad, and Mahayana Buddhism the creative products of *later* centuries, it is also the case that the religious experiences centred upon the Buddha, Confucius, the Hebrew prophets, the Upanishads, and the Ionian philosophers that *did* emerge in the Axial Age evolved in ways that were surprising and unique in the centuries that were to follow. Thus the great religious traditions evolved distinctively and creatively. Anyone who supposes that all religions are the same or that each religion remains the same is lacking in historical sensitivity. It is not even the case that the religious traditions of our four areas were giving different answers to the same questions, they were asking different questions because they were perceiving the world through different lenses. To understand others it is necessary in some degree to see the world through *their* eyes in the light of *their* questions as they emerged in *their* history. It is the failure of Christian theology to realise this that has caused a number of her present problems in relation to world religions.

(iv) This failure has been compounded by a fourth factor that surfaced during the period we are analysing. We surmised earlier that our four areas of Europe, the Middle East, India, and China developed during this period in a more or less equal, more or less separate and more or less parallel fashion. The separate nature of their development must be qualified. In the case of Christian Europe, that separation and isolation were almost total. After the conversion of Constantine and the eventual rise of Islam, Christianity developed its unique institutions in a 'closed' Europe which, in its isolated state, tolerated only one religious choice, namely Christianity. Nowhere else was this isolation so absolute. Islam, which inherited and continued the exclusivistic approach exemplified in Christianity, advanced within fifty years after the death of Muhammad as far west as Spain and as far east as India. In so doing

it was forced into contact with other religious traditions and civilisations outside the Middle East. The test case was the Muslim incursion into India where it entered into a clash with a different world view[8]. The Muslim world view stressed revelation, the prophet, denunciation of error, Allah as the one, transcendent and creator God, truth as one, salvation as personal, heaven and hell as real places, man as a body/soul unity, and a religious experience of God; the Indian world view (whether Hindu or Buddhist) stressed revelation in a different sense, interiority, tolerance, the immortal ground of the soul, emanation, truth as many-sided, different paths to salvation, rebirth, the self as inward or illusory, and a religious experience of nature, self, and the Absolute as well as of God. Islam was therefore plunged 'willy nilly' into an awareness of other religions denied to Christianity.

The case of China was even more dramatic although the process was slower and quieter. Into that most self-sufficient of lands came a foreign intrusion, namely the Buddhist tradition of India. The story of the spread of Buddhism from India into China and thence into much of the rest of East Asia is one of the great missionary stories of history[3]. China and Chinese religion were radically different from India and Indian Buddhism. The Sanskrit language was different from Chinese; Buddhist monks sat lightly to family relationships which were crucial for China; Buddhists thought in terms of rebirth according to one's deeds whereas the Chinese had little interest in the afterlife; Buddhists recognised while downgrading the Hindu pantheon of deities whereas the Chinese had little interest in *any* deities; Buddhist monks formed an extraordinary norm beyond politics and society whereas Chinese religion, Confucian and even Taoist, was essentially an attempt to solve political and social problems. The Buddhists, through skilful preaching, translation and adaptation to changing circumstances, introduced and indigenised Mahayana Buddhism (notably Zen and Pure Land) within China so that it became part of the San Chiao, the three traditions, of China. For Europe and Christianity, however, the isolation from outside influence was more complete.

(v) Fifthly, during the long centuries we have considered, it is possible to conceptualise periods and movements that transcend the separateness of our four areas. The Axial Age itself ending about 350 BC had been one such period. From 350 BC to about 200 AD there was another period in which there was the simultaneous rise of devotional religion in Christianity, Mahayana Buddhism and Bhakti Hinduism; there was also the appearance of recognisable religious traditions that we can meaningfully call Christian, Jewish, Hindu, Buddhist and Chinese (with Han Confucianism). From about 200 to 600 AD there was another period in which there was the missionary spread of Christianity throughout the Roman Empire, Buddhism throughout China, Hinduism throughout India and into South East Asia, and Zoroastrianism in Sassanid Persia. With the emergence of Islam in the seventh century AD and the virtual demise of Zoroastrianism, the religious contours of the world became more recognisable in present-day terms and another period began. From the seventh century AD until the sixteenth century AD, the evolution of the main religious traditions within their separate regions was so similar that overall movements appeared in different parts of the world at the same time[10]. For example, the period ending about 1250 AD saw the simultaneous emergence of great philosophical/theological syntheses within Christianity, Islam, Judaism, Hinduism, and neo-Confucian China through the work of Aquinas and Bonaventure, al-Ghazali, Maimonides, Ramanuja, and Chu Hsi; the fourteenth century AD saw the worldwide appearance of significant forms of mysticism in Eastern Christianity, Western Christianity, Judaism, Islam, Buddhism and Hinduism; and the sixteenth century AD witnessed the rise of vernacular devotional fervour among Protestant Christians, devotional Hindus, Shi'ite Muslims, and the newly emerging Sikhs, as well as Pure Land Buddhists.

(f) The Rise of the West: 16th century AD to 1945. During that same sixteenth century AD another movement began which was destined by 1945 to draw the various civilisations and religions of the world into closer contact and mutual awareness. We may

term it the age of the 'rise of the West'[11]. For, with the sea-borne explorations of Spanish and Portuguese and later Dutch and British navigators, Europe abandoned its isolation and entered with a vengeance into new contact with older civilis-ations and fresh discoveries of new civilisations. Vasco da Gama got round the Cape of Good Hope to India and opened the way to the East Indies and China, Columbus discovered a new world in America. Captain Cook later uncovered another new continent in Australasia, and eventually the interior of Africa was also opened up. Christian missions followed and occasionally accompanied these voyages of discovery. Although a long succession of Christian mission-aries, from Las Casas in the sixteenth century to C F Andrews in the twentieth, have endeavoured to distance the Christian tradition from Western civilisation, in practical terms the two have often gone hand in hand. The scientific and industrial revolutions gave Western civilisation a decisive technological advantage over others and it so happened that the early modern period of Western cultural and religious energy coincided with a time of relative lethargy in most of the other world civilisations and religions. The time of more or less equal, parallel, and separate civilisations was passing away. One region, the West, together with its religious tradition, Christianity, now had a noticeable advantage over the others. Thus it was that the new continents that were discovered, the Americas, Australasia, and Southern Africa, became Chris-tian continents. The local religions of those areas, the Mayas, Incas, Aztecs, and the various primal religions, were absorbed, destroyed, or restricted in influence. Christianity had great success with and has a deep responsibility for the primal religious areas of the world[12]. Her direct influence over the major religions of the other great civilisations was less. Although missions were established sooner or later in India, China, Japan, the East Indies, and other areas of Asia and the Middle East, there were relatively few converts from the Muslim, Hindu, Buddhist, or Chinese traditions. Instead reform movements arose within Islam, Judaism, Hinduism and Buddhism in response to the twin challenges of the West and Christianity. These reform movements eventually became associated with growing nationalism, especially in areas under colonial government. Meanwhile, back in a Europe that had now propagated itself by white emigration to the Americas, Australasia and southern Africa, a divide was beginning to open up between the Christian Church, already fragmented by the Reformation, and a culture increasingly influenced by humanistic, nationalistic and scientific values. By 1945, twin suspicions were starting to form in some Christian minds. On the one hand the spectacular triumph on a world scale of the western scientific model had brought material benefits to the world and was beginning to transform it into a vast global town in which all nations were coming closer to each other; on the other hand it had also led to two European world wars which illustrated the spiritual weakness of the West and prompted thinkers such as Bonhoeffer to talk in terms of the emergence of a 'post-Christian age'. Within the Christian community it was becoming evident to some that although the church was nominally a world church present in all corners of the earth, it was also a divided, traditional and shallow church which had unwittingly tolerated the sundering within the western consciousness of a sense of God, humanity, and nature and therefore opened up the possibility of this split in consciousness being exported elsewhere along with the Gospel it was proclaiming. In short the so-called world church was still a western church which had yet to grapple theologically with the world situation and to prophesy theologically about the disintegration within western culture. Although other religious traditions were successfully renewing themselves by 1945, the form of their renewal was often influenced by the same questions, namely should they repudiate Christianity and western thought, should they accept one without the other, should they accept something of both, and should they strive to help the West and Christianity in their present predicament?

(g) The present global age. From 1945 to the present-day constitutes the final, global stage in the history of religion. It is a complicated era that is difficult to interpret because we are acting in the play rather than observing it from afar. No one civilisation is dominant in the sense that the West was dominant prior to the Second World War. Although it is clear

that we live in 'one world' which is becoming a vast global city, it is a plural world with plural religions. In the cultural/political sense, the West remains important; the Communist block that has formed around the Soviet Union is significant; the Muslim world has emerged in stature since the oil crisis; the Far Eastern countries of Japan and China are important in different but perhaps complementary ways; India and Israel are significant Third World areas for contrasting reasons. Religiously, Christianity remains important, although she is expanding more rapidly in South America and Africa and outside Europe than in Europe; Communism has emerged as a quasi-religion with its own sects; there has been a renaissance of the Hindu, Buddhist and Muslim traditions in India, South East Asia and the Middle East; the Jews have found a homeland after the trauma of the Holocaust; and the Confucian and Taoist traditions of the Far East and primal religions everywhere have diminished in influence. In spite of the formation of new religious groups such as the Baha'is, the new religions of Japan, and the many African indigenous churches it is the major religious traditions together with the quasi-religion of Communism that remain the dominant factors. Each of them have become more universal so that not only Christians but also Hindus, Buddhists, Muslims and Jews (and Communists) have at least a minimal presence in most parts of the world.

(i) In the present global religious situation, three other matters are worthy of brief attention. In the first place, there is a relatively greater religious concern for human beings and their life on this earth than for the life of the world to come. As Robert Bellah puts it:

'I expect traditional religious symbolism to be maintained and developed in new directions, but with growing awareness that it is symbolism and that man in the last analysis is responsible for the choice of his symbolism.'[13]

Bellah's imagery is western, and indeed American, and it may be doubted whether individual choice in the western sense is globally available; but it is true to say that a concern for history, this world, human progress, social improvement, and humanity's global future are increasingly on the religious agenda of all the major traditions.

(ii) Secondly, there is a growing global awareness that each religious tradition and the human race in general must bring together three elements that have increasingly become separated in human consciousness, namely transcendence, humankind, and nature. Modern science, with its concentration upon and research into nature, has been partly responsible for this split of consciousness. The ideological roots of modern science with its interest in nature and specialisation lie partly in Christian theology with its 'Hebrew' hierarchy of transcendence (God) at the top, humanity in the middle, and nature at the bottom, and its 'Greek' penchant for logical analysis of different elements into their discrete parts. Primal religion, Hinduism, Buddhism and Chinese religion have held together in a more integral fashion this triple awareness of transcendence, humanity and nature. However, it is not a question of apportioning praise or blame, though Christians have much to learn from others about integral thinking, as we shall see. It is vital that all religions should not only take nature more seriously, give due regard to humanity in its multi-faceted complexity, and recapture a vision of transcendence but also integrate the three together more closely in their concern for the planet and its human family.

(iii) Thirdly, religious dialogue between the major religious traditions is seen to be increasingly urgent for general as well as religious reasons. Within the perspective of global history, the West can no longer view the rest of the world as a backdrop to its own supremacy, China can no longer analyse others merely through the binoculars of its own Great Wall, Communism can no longer construe the world through a monolithic communist perspective, and Islam can no longer look out from its holy places of Mecca and Medina upon a religious world divided neatly into *dar al-Islam* (lands of Islam) and *dar al-harb* (territory outside Islam). Hindu gurus officiate in Boston and London as well as India, a Burmese Buddhist has presided over the

United Nations as its Secretary-General, and it is reasonable to assume that before long there may well be a Pope from the Third World. From now on history, both general and religious, will be increasingly global rather than parochial. No religion, no culture, is an island. Global concerns affect all. And yet our time of global danger is also our time of global opportunity. The great religions of the world are open to each other as never before. They meet not according to the laws of geographical proximity as from 500 BC to 1500 AD, nor according to the dictates of western and Christian imperatives as from 1500 to 1945 AD, but in genuine dialogue on issues of urgent global significance.

(h) Religion in the future. We do not know what the future history of religion will be. Basically there are four possibilities. One is that religions as we have known them will wither away before the onslaught of secularisation. Secularisation theorists differ among themselves concerning this. However, if religiousness is part of human nature, *it* (i.e. human nature) cannot wither away and the question then remains what concrete form will religiousness take? So far the major religions have proved flexibly tenacious, and Communism for all its rapid spread has the hallmarks of a corrective and addition to the 'religious' scene rather than a substitute for all that has gone before. Another possibility is that the major religions will join together in an ecumenical movement that will seek to form one global religion encompassing the best elements of the traditions that have so far been separate entities. For the foreseeable future this appears to be an unlikely hypothesis. Another possibility is that one of the present religions will fulfil all the others and come to dominate them all. There is no doubt that religious traditions will continue to make converts from each other, and that religious contexts will continue to change in different parts of the world. It may even be the case that a completely new religion could arise and spread in spectacular fashion. Indeed some would argue that Communism fits into this category. As we shall see a prominent Christian theological approach adopts the fulfilment stance and claims that Christianity is the crown,

the fulfilment, of the other religions. However other religions have their own fulfilment theories, and it is one thing statically to state a fulfilment approach, it is another thing actually to practice it in terms of the cosmic process. The fourth possibility is that the major religious traditions will renew themselves through dialogue with each other and with the global currents of the present age. This dialogue does not advance on the assumption that it is an intellectual discourse conducted in a relaxed atmosphere of basic agreement upon presuppositions. Dialogue does not necessarily presuppose underlying assent to a given set of principles[14]. It proceeds on the hypothesis that religious traditions may differ as well as agree in regard to basic matters of commitment, spirituality, and world view. It rejoices in the fact that one can learn from dialogue and deepen one's tradition in the process of theological and spiritual concourse with others. However, the aim of dialogue is not for one religion to become a carbon copy of another. The goal is that through dialogue there should be deeper mutual understanding between religions, and the opportunity for a tradition so to renew itself that it may respond to and indeed help to create a global atmosphere within which the planetary human family might prosper.

It is clear that so rapid a survey begs many questions of both fact and interpretation. It is clear also that it paints a more comprehensive picture of the history of religion than is often sketched for the Christian theologian who, as often as not, views religious history through the restricted horizon of the Old and New Testaments.

2. A MODEL FOR UNDERSTANDING WORLD RELIGIONS

So far we have concentrated upon the historical development of world religions. This must remain central and any attempts at further understanding must start from this historical base. In this section, we offer for consideration a model for understanding world religions that uses the historical data we have alluded to but cuts a cross-section through these data in order to give us a better grasp of each major religion and of the conceptual framework lying behind them all. Although this model can be applied more widely, we will restrict it, in our present analysis, to the great living religions of Christianity, Islam, Judaism, Hinduism, and Buddhism that lie at the core of our book.

(a) In the first place, all the major religious traditions of the world contain eight inter-linked elements. The major religions are dynamic organisms within which there are eight inter-acting dimensions; they are historical chains within which there are eight connecting links. The eight links are those of religious community, ritual, ethics, social involvement, scripture/myth, concept, aesthetics, and spirituality. All major religions have some sort of religious community, they all engage in different forms of worship, lying behind them all are certain ethical norms, they are all involved in social and political outreach within the wider community, sacred texts and myths are important for them all, they all emphasise particular clusters of doctrines, they all produce religious art and sculpture, and they all infer distinctive modes of spirituality. In other words there are eight common elements within the great world religions and it is a great help to be aware of this for they provide pegs upon which knowledge can be hung.

(b) However these elements are present in separate traditions with different weights and different emphases. Because all religions have these elements this does not mean that they are all the same. Thus all the major religions have their *communities*: Christians the church with its various denomi-nations, Muslims the *ummah* with its Sunni and Shi'ite bran-ches, Jews their own community with its Orthodox, Reform and Conservative wings, Hindus their *sampradayas* (sects) within the wider whole of the caste system, and Buddhists the *sangha* (monastic community) with its Theravada and Mahayana schools. Religious communities are common to all these traditions, the nature of religious communities varies between them. Likewise there is a *ritual and worship element* in all religions. Each has pilgrimages and festivals based upon its own holy places and sacred times; each has *rites de passage* connected with birth, initiation, marriage, and death; and

each has particular patterns of worship—church services, mosque prayers, synagogue celebrations, temple ceremonies, and pagoda observances. The fact of ritual and worship is common, the nature of ritual and worship differs between religions. Moreover, all religions contain an *ethical stance*: Christians stress love and service, Muslims and Jews stress the Shari'ah and the Torah (legal ethics in its widest sense), Hindus and Buddhists stress the Dharma (viewed more transcendentally by the Buddhists but involving nature as well as man in both). Ethics is therefore common, but its application differs. Equally all religious traditions have their *patterns of social and political involvement*: the diverse relationships between church and state in Christianity, the close connection between the state and *ummah* in Islam, the alternation between exile and religious nationalism in Judaism, the social conformity of the caste system but relative indifference to politics in Hinduism, and the close social involvement of Theravada and more flexible involvement of Mahayana Buddhism. Social involvement is common, its forms vary. *Scriptures and myths* are also universal throughout the major religions: Christians, Muslims and Jews stress one sacred text, the Bible, the Koran, and the Jewish Bible; Hindus view the Veda (an umbrella scripture containing the four Vedas, Brahmanas, Aranyakas and Upanishads) as the revealed scripture that is heard (*shruti*), and give subordinate status to other sacred texts that are remembered (*smriti*); Theravada Buddhists recognise the massive Pali Canon to which the Mahayana Buddhists add the Mahayana Sutras. Scripture and the myths connected with sacred texts are therefore common, but the view of scripture and the status of myths vary. Clearly all religious traditions have *concepts* that are important to them: Christianity, Islam and Judaism agree that there is one God and yet differ in the details of their monotheism; Hindus and Buddhists agree that we do not live one life but are continually reborn, but they differ as to the nature of ultimate reality and the self. Religious concepts and ideas may therefore be universally present but they are hardly the same. Furthermore, *aesthetic elements* are present in all religions whether in the form of architecture, painting, music, literature, or dancing, yet attitudes towards them vary. The monotheistic religions have a tendency to occasional iconoclasm whereas the eastern religions glory in luxuriant imagery, and the variety in shape between churches, mosques, synagogues, temples and pagodas is illustrative of difference as well as similarity. And finally all religions share common modes of *spirituality* related to mysticism, devotion, ritual awe, and consecrated service yet they differ in the balance and weight given to them. In short, all religions contain the eight elements we have outlined, albeit in different measures, and with different emphases, and therefore comparative religious communities, comparative worship, comparative ethics, comparative cultural attitudes, comparative scripture, comparative doctrines, comparative aesthetics, and comparative spirituality become authentic possibilities. A combination of the twin truths, that all religions have these elements yet have them in different measure, provides a framework of understanding that allows for both similarity and difference.

(c) Just as importantly for our purposes, the model we have outlined gives us an insight into each of the major living religions. For example it is helpful to realise that the Hindu sects, the worship in Hindu temples, Hindu ethical codes, the caste system, the Veda and later scriptural tradition, the Hindu concepts of Brahman, Atman, reincarnation and so on, classical Hindu dance and music, and spiritual modes such as yoga are not a chaotic jumble but are inter-linked. They give meaning to each other in the developing organism that we call the Hindu tradition. Let us pause for a moment to glance at the major traditions in the light of our eight elements. We may say, in passing, that it is a valuable grid whereby we may understand Christianity but as the major concern of our later chapters will be with Christian theology we will concentrate now upon the other four major religions.

(i) The *religious community* of Islam is the *ummah*. It has a less particular meaning than the Christian church and the reason for this dates back, like so many other elements in Islam, to the beginnings of that tradition. When Muhammad was in Mecca his group of Muslims was in a similar position to that of the early Christians; he was the leader of a band of followers suspected by the wider

community. But when he moved to Medina he became not only the religious but also the political, cultural and even military leader of the Muslims there so that the term *ummah* received a wider than religious connotation. It is significant that the start of the Muslim dating system goes back not to 610 AD when Muhammad began to receive the revelations that later formed the Koran but to 622 AD when he moved from Mecca to Medina where *ummah* and state, religion and society became almost one. Muslim *ritual* centres upon two of the five pillars of Islam, the *salat*, prayer five times daily in the direction of Mecca, and the Haj, the annual pilgrimage to Mecca which is a unifying symbol and a lifetime ambition for all Muslims. The Muslim *ethical code* became centred upon the Shari'ah, a series of ethical regulations derived from the Koran, the sayings of Muhammad, and the law schools, and important in it were two more of the five pillars of Islam, namely almsgiving, and the annual monthly fast of Ramadan, another symbol of unity and also a real discipline if the daytime temperature is over 100 degrees Fahrenheit! As we have already suggested, Muslim *social and political involvement* is usually considerable, and Muslims find it hard to live in a state like India that is not run by Muslims. The Koran, the Muslim *scripture*, enshrined the revelations that are authoritative in Muslim tradition because they are taken to have been revealed by Allah directly to man *through* Muhammad. A fifth pillar of Islam, the confession of faith, lies at the heart of Muslim *belief*, 'Allah is Allah, and Muhammad is his prophet' summarises the message of the early verses of the Koran to the effect that the One God requires praise and right living from men and Muhammad is his warner about the judgement or paradise to come in virtue of man's response. This stress upon the One God led Islam to prohibit God's representation in art form, and prompted the development of calligraphy, mosque decoration, and the other facets of Muslim *aesthetics*. The somewhat austere nature of mainstream Muslim *spirituality* which stressed obedience to and worship of a transcendent just God promoted by reaction the rise of a warm Sufi mystical spirituality that related back to mystical strains within Muhammad himself. It can readily be seen that the eight elements of Islam we have briefly described shed light in an integral fashion upon Islam as a whole.

(ii) When we turn to Judaism we find that their *religious community*, like that of Islam, is closely related to the wider community. Indeed it is notoriously difficult to separate the religious from the ethnic within the Jewish tradition. The reason for this is closely related to Jewish history in which a stress upon God's election of the Jewish people has been accompanied by tragic periods of exile and suffering which have only served to underline the uniqueness of the Jews as a people. Jewish *worship* takes place on the sabbath, made sacred by God himself, in synagogues that became necessary when the original temple was 'lost', and Jewish festivals commemorate important events in Jewish history such as the Exodus. Jewish *ethics* centre upon the Torah which has mediated ethical and social norms. Unlike the other religions we are considering, the Jews did not create a great civilisation. Indeed their religious genius was to survive in other civilisations against all the odds. From the exile of the sixth century BC to 1948 AD, and especially during the medieval ordeal, their *involvement* in wider society was often that of undergoing persecution at the hands of the civilisation in which they lived. This could be justified theologically by the notion that they were God's Suffering Servant elected by God to be the suffering heart of mankind, but the mixed blessing of emancipation followed by the horrors of the Holocaust rendered this theodicy threadbare and present-day Israel has reacted in the opposite direction. The Jewish Bible is the Jewish *scripture* supplemented by the Mishnah and Talmud, and the Jewish concepts derive from them. They overlap with a number of Christian and Muslim *concepts* except of course in regard to Christ, the Trinity and Muhammad, and they tend to particularise Jewish concerns such as the role of the Messiah. *Aesthetically*, like the Muslims, Jews have been influenced by the prescriptions against graven images so that their liturgy itself has become one of their aesthetic glories. Like the Muslims they too have produced *mystical shoots* in the Kabbalah and Hasidism to supplement the stress upon obedience to an awesome personal God. In many ways similar to the Muslims—in their spirituality, aesthetic aspirations, emphasis upon legal ethics, non-trinitarian monotheism, and community spirit—the Jews have lacked the Muslim missionary spirit. They have looked for a Messiah who was to come rather than a prophet who had already arrived, and their origins and ethos have constrained them to survive gloriously within and contribute to other civilisations rather than create one of their own.

(iii) The Hindus lacked a founder and this was one of the reasons why there is no strong sense of a Hindu *religious community* as such. There is no 'church' or 'orthodoxy'. Instead there are many *sampradayas* (sects) which focus upon different objects of worship including Shiva, the Goddess, and Vishnu with his various *avataras* (incarnations) notably Rama and Krishna. Many Hindus belong to no religious community as such, and others owe their allegiance to local gurus with small followings. *Worship* is accordingly variegated and somewhat chaotic. The Hindu sacraments and daily worship centre upon the home. Hindus may visit many temples which are open for worship every day, and they may attend festivals associated with many different gods. Hindu *ethics* encourage good actions, and they support the maxim of the Bhagavad Gita that one should do one's duty because it is right and without thought of reward. Hindu ethics are inevitably linked to Hindu notions of *social involvement* and these, in their turn, hinge upon the question of caste. One is involved in wider society through one's status in the caste system, and one's status in the caste system is determined by one's deeds, good or bad, according to which one is reborn at the end of each earthly life. Because the caste system, although in flux now, has provided social stability and security to the Hindu, there has been less need for political power to reside fully in Hindu hands. It is significant not only that Hindus have lived under Buddhist, Muslim and British rule but also that independent India is a secular state by comparison

with Pakistan which became a Muslim state. Like Hindu worship and beliefs, Hindu views of *scripture* are also flexible. In theory the original Rig Veda is the fountainhead of sacred texts. In fact the Rig Veda, along with the other three Vedas, and the Brahmanas, Aranyakas and Upanishads, is part of a wider corpus collectively known as the Veda. In practice Hindus tend to refer back to the later parts of this collective Veda such as the Upanishads, and the important Vedanta schools comment upon the Upanishads (which are part of the Veda) and the Vedanta Sutras and the Bhagavad Gita (which are not) in working out their systems of thought. It is therefore not surprising that Hindu concepts and deities are many and diverse in view of the variety of sacred texts, forms of worship and religious communities. Indeed even when the Vedanta commentators interpret the *same* texts they find in them five different theological and philosophical positions ranging from a radical dualism between God, humanity, and the world in Dvaita Vedanta to an ultimate non-dualism between God, humanity and the world in Advaita Vedanta. Yet underlying the diversity there are certain basic *concepts*, however differently interpreted: Brahman as the ultimate Reality behind the universe, the Atman as the real inner self of man, the human lot as continual rebirth, salvation as release from the round of rebirths through realisation of one's real nature in regard to Brahman. Every *aesthetic approach* known to humans has been utilised by Hindus to represent the diversity of religious truth within this overarching pattern. By contrast with the graceful simplicity and ordered vision of a Muslim mosque, or the soaring spire of a Christian church reaching up towards a personally known transcendence, a Hindu temple mirrors the Hindu aesthetics and the Hindu vision with its ornate structure, its many-crannied complexity, its different levels, and its elaborate yet attractive series of rooms and rooves. Hindu *spirituality* is also varied as can be seen in the Bhagavad Gita with its three ways of inward realisation through yoga, devotional trust in a personal God, and serving one's fellows and God in the world without hope of reward. Again our eight elements give an inter-connected view of the religious tradition we call Hinduism.

(iv) The Buddhist tradition by contrast is in some ways simpler than the Hindu but insofar as it has spread into many different cultures throughout South East Asia it too has appeared in many varied forms. The main *religious community* of the Buddhists is the *sangha*, the order of monks, and it represents the spiritual, exemplary, and often intellectual élite. Although more important in the Theravada branch of the Buddhist tradition than in the Mahayana which stressed more the role of laymen, the *sangha* remains of universal significance. Although there are *rituals* of many sorts, including pagoda prayers and the ceremony of initiation which often re-enacts the going-out of the Buddha from the security and wealth of his palace into the suffering world where he would eventually find enlightenment, Buddhist worship *par excellence* is found in meditation of one sort or another. *Ethics* too are important in seeking enlightenment, and the non-violence that lies at their core refers not only to human beings (the Buddhist world has a good record in regard to peace) but also to nature which is in continuity with the human world. The Theravada world centred upon Sri Lanka, Thailand and Burma has maintained the vision of a Buddhist society led by Buddhist leaders, exemplified in Buddhist monks, and involving Buddhist laymen; the Mahayana Buddhist world centred upon China and Japan has been more ready to settle for *social and political involvement* with others in multi-religious civilisations. The Theravada *scripture*, the Pali Canon, contains not only stories and teaching of the Buddha but also monastic precepts and philosophical ideas, and these are supplemented among Mahayana Buddhists by the Mahayana Sutras. Buddhists stress the *concepts*, the Dharma, of the Buddha because they represent eternal truth that was uncovered (rather than brilliantly conceived) by him. Together with the Buddha and the *sangha*, the Dharma is one of the three central Refuges (or pillars) of Buddhism. Even so concepts, doctrines, teachings remain a second-order activity by comparison with the Christian

stress upon theological doctrine. The four Noble Truths of the Buddha—that this world is a fleeting world of suffering, that our selfish nature binds us to rebirth into this world of suffering, that our destiny is to escape from this world of suffering into the bliss of nirvana, and that salvation lies in following the eightfold path of the Buddha—these truths, although important, are secondary, they are a means to an end. Buddhist *aesthetics*, although multi-faceted, centres above all upon sculpture and architecture. Everywhere around the Buddhist world there are carvings of the Buddha which illustrate the way one should follow. Especially interesting are his hand-gestures (*mudras*): the Buddha raises his right hand to ward off evil and cast out fear, he places hand upon hand to symbolise the importance of meditation, he forms a wheel with his fingers to refer to his Dharma, he holds out his hand as if to receive a gift to suggest that anyone can go to him for help, and he points his hand to the earth to bear witness that he will not forsake it in its hour of need. In the realm of *spirituality*, Buddhists have stressed above all the practice of meditation. Huston Smith has said that Christians believe in God, Buddhists believe in meditation. In fact all religions acknowledge that meditation can help but it is chiefly the Buddhists who have translated theory about meditation into practice.

(d)(i) The eight elements we have described above are an important part of our model. However, lying behind them is something that is even more important, namely transcendent reality. For a Christian this would be God, for a Muslim Allah, for a Jew Yahweh, for a Hindu Brahman, and for a Buddhist Nirvana. Insofar as it is transcendent this reality is less clear than the eight elements we have analysed. They are directly observable, transcendence is not.

(ii) However transcendent reality is made more clear by means of a mediating focus that lies at the heart of each religious tradition. This mediating focus—Christ for a Christian, the Koran for a Muslim, the Torah for a Jew, a personal deity or the Atman for a Hindu, and the Buddha or the Dharma for a Buddhist—brings transcendent reality closer and makes it more meaningful. God is therefore mediated through Christ, Allah through the Koran, Yahweh through the Torah, Brahman through a Hindu Lord or the Atman within, and Nirvana through the Buddha or the Dharma. It is this combination of a transcendent reality and a mediating focus that lies behind and gives meaning to the eight elements of each religious tradition.

(e) To complete our model we must add one more ingredient. This ingredient is crucial. It lies within humankind, and although it is difficult to pin down in one word it is vital for it gives life, pattern and shape to the whole. For some person, and indeed some group of persons, has to respond to mediated reality. Persons have dynamically to use the eight elements that form a tradition otherwise those elements are lifeless forms. The quality whereby persons do this, the religious intention that breathes life into a tradition and makes transcendence real, is elusive to grasp and understand. This quality, like transcendence, cannot be seen. It is intangible yet it is perhaps also the clue to everything else. For without it there would be no religions with their eight elements to study. In short, persons and their intentions matter. It is the intentions of men and women who are Christian, Muslim, Jewish, Hindu and Buddhist that enable the Christian, Muslim, Jewish, Hindu and Buddhist traditions to continue and to vibrate. Human intentions, perhaps we can say human faith, are the final key to our model.

It is my contention that by means of this model we can come to a reasonable understanding of the religious traditions of the world. Fully to understand others requires one more step. This involves 'passing over' into other traditions in order to 'be there' before returning with renewed vision to one's own tradition. We will take this final step later when we attempt to see what Christian theology can learn from other religions.

FOOTNOTES

1. L H Jordan, *Comparative Religion: Its Genesis and Growth*, Edinburgh, 1905, p 163.

2. Richard E Leakey, *The Making of Mankind*, Book Club Associates, London, 1981, p 40.

3. See J Maringer, *The Gods of Prehistoric Man*, Alfred A Knopf, New York, 1960; A. Leroi-Gourhan, *Les Religions de la Préhistoire*, Presses Universitaires de France, Paris, 1971.

4. C Darwin, *The Descent of Man and Selection in Relation to Sex*, John Murray, London, 1901, p 143.

5. M Eliade, *The Quest*, University of Chicago Press, Chicago, 1971, p 70.

6. W H McNeill, *The Rise of the West*, New American Library, New York, 1963, p 52.

7. In recent scholarship Zoroaster's dates have been put back before the sixth century BC. See M Boyce, *A History of Zoroastrianism*, Vol 1, E J Brill, Leiden, 1975.

8. The classic account of this clash appears in R C Zaehner, (ed), *A Concise Encyclopaedia of Living Faiths*, Hutchinson, London, 1959, p xi–xxi (Introduction).

9. An early lucid account is in Arthur F Wright, *Buddhism in Chinese History*, Atheneum, New York, 1968.

10. See F Whaling, 'Comparative Approaches to the Study of Religion: Global History as a Basis for Comparison' pp 243–255 in F Whaling (ed), *Contemporary Approaches to the Study of Religion*, vol 1, Mouton, Berlin New York Amsterdam, 1984.

11. W H McNeill entitles his book on global history *The Rise of the West* (New American Library, New York, 1963) which is to highlight the era of global history from the sixteenth century AD to 1945 but to do less than justice to the rest.

12. A straightforward account of the spread of Christian missions is S Neill, *A History of Christian Missions*, Penguin, Harmondsworth, 1964.

13. Robert Bellah, '*Religious Evolution*', p 49 in W A Lessa and E Z Vogt, *Reader in comparative religion*, Harper and Row, New York, 1972 Paperback.

14. Dialogue will be discussed in chapter four. See also F Whaling, *An Approach to Dialogue: Christianity and Hinduism*, Lucknow Publishing House, Lucknow, 1966.

15. This model will be amplified in my J N Pal Lectures in Religion at Calcutta University in March 1985 to be published under the title *Comparative Religion*.

CHAPTER THREE

CHRISTIAN THEOLOGY AND THE DEVELOPMENT OF THE WORD 'THEOLOGY'[1]

The word 'theology' can be and is used in a number of different ways. It has developed a variety of meanings, such that the use of this same word to allude to different concepts sometimes leads to confusion. In this chapter I intend to look at the development of the word 'theology' and in the course of this analysis, certain suggestions will be made that will help to provide a framework for our discussion of Christian theology and world religions.

I. THE GREEK USE OF THE WORD 'THEOLOGIA'

Our modern word 'theology' is derived from the Greek word *theologia*. Our first task is to investigate the development of the word *theologia* in pre-Christian western thought.

(a) Account of the gods or God. The first and main meaning of the Greek word *theologia* is that it signifies an account of the gods or God. In Liddell and Scott's *Greek–English Lexicon* two hundred and thirty-three derivatives of *theos* are quoted, ranging from *theoblabeia* (infatuation sent by the gods) to *theocrestos* (delivered by God) and *theoō* (to deify).[2] Only eleven of these derivatives are not connected with the gods or God, and in some cases this is merely because the words have become secularised to designate the name of a city, an eyesalve, etc. Theology, then, for the Greeks and ever since has been centred upon the gods or God. The gods or God with whom theology has to do have varied according to time and place; the fact that theology has to do with God, however

conceptualised, has not varied. As far as the Greeks, and indeed the Romans, were concerned the gods were to be found mainly in their pantheon: Zeus (or Jupiter), Hera (or Juno), Apollo (or Phoebus), Ares (or Mars), Poseidon (or Neptune), Aphrodite (or Venus), Hermes (or Mercury), Athene (or Minerva), Artemis (or Diana), Hades (or Pluto). *Theologia* was an account of the gods, and even up to the fifth century AD it was common to describe the early poets such as Orpheus, Hesiod, Musaeus, and Homer as theologians. The gods described by these poets were polytheistic and anthropomorphic; they were not creator gods nor ethically righteous; they were dependent upon a higher fate; and yet within these limits they influenced the world and men. Within the Greek world view they mediated transcendence.

(b) The Stoics. The Stoics later developed the view that three kinds of *theologia* can be distinguished, namely mythical *theologia*, natural or rational *theologia*, and civil *theologia*.[3] Mythical *theologia* corresponds to the accounts of the gods of the pantheon that we have been describing; civil *theologia* designates the knowledge of the due rites and ceremonies of the gods that were so important to the Romans; natural or rational *theologia* became increasingly important in Hellenistic times as a precursor of what we would call philosophy of religion. Thus early was theology seen to be a generic term which included systematic description, practical exposition, and philosophising upon the nature of God.

(c) Philosophical theology. The latter philosophical concept of theology was destined to become very important in later Greek thought and it was destined to have an important influence upon Christian theology in later times. This development of *theologia* as philosophical theology mirrored certain developments within Greek thought itself. From Aeschylus onwards, there was a tendency to identify the gods and assume the possibility of their convergence into one divine being. For the philosophers, this divine being was often rationalised, moralised, and spiritualised, and viewed nonpersonally as 'World Reason', 'the Divine', or 'Being'. As such this divine being influenced the world as a power giving order and meaning.[4] A parallel but somewhat less philo-

sophical development within Hellenistic syncretism involved a process of assimilation between Greek and non-Greek divinities whereby the same divine entities were seen to lie behind the names of different gods, especially Isis. One godhead was seen to be the divine All. In neo-Platonic thought, the divine was conceived as the universal One, as Being itself with hypostases and emanations.[5] *Theologia* was then seen as involving an account of God, however conceived, as well as the gods. It was the notion of *theologia* as relating to God that was adopted by Christian theology although of course particular content was given to the meaning of the word 'God'. In general we may anticipate by saying that *theologia* as relating to the gods was destined to become the discipline of mythology, and the term *theologia qua* theology was destined to be reserved for considerations involving transcendent Being. Thus the question of whether Marxism has a theology does not hinge so much upon whether Marxism includes the eight elements of religion we looked at in the last chapter (which it does) but rather upon whether Marxism has a transcendent Focus which can be theologised.

(d) Theology in relation to philosophy. Having stated this, we must insert a rider in relation to the Greek view of *theologia*. In Greek philosophical theology the stress was placed upon philosophy rather than theology as later understood. Indeed Aristotle divided the theoretical forms of philosophy into three—mathematical, physical, and theological—the last being what we would designate as metaphysics which included his doctrine of the divine nature and of God as unmoved Mover. Plato's method involved a demythologising of the Greek poets and it also gave the primacy to more philosophical considerations. The Stoics likewise distinguished between the theology of the poets and the philosophical interpretation arising therefrom. The question was thus raised in early times of the relationship between theology and philosophy. Are they separate disciplines? Is one the handmaid of the other, and if so which is the handmaid of which? Are theology and philosophy of religion complementary or opposed or in dialectical relationship? In Christian theology the Hebrew content of God would replace the Greek

mythical theology but Greek philosophical categories would be used to conceptualise the Hebrew content of God as seen ' in Christ.

(e) Theology part of a wider whole. One final point remains to be made before we leave the Greek use of the word *theologia*. *Theologia* in either its mythical or rational form was not seen as an end in itself. It was subordinate to the Graeco-Roman dominant educational model of *humanitas*, what we would call the Humanities or Liberal Arts.[6] The main stress in this model was upon literature and humanity. There was resistance to the notion of elevating *theologia* or philosophy into a 'discipline' independent of humankind's general literary-humanistic social and political concerns. The danger was that the 'discipline' would become a specialisation in its own right and if that were to happen truth would be seen to lie not in humanity or in the public weal but in the 'discipline' as an intellectual pursuit independent of its practical influence upon humanity and public affairs. In a classic phrase, Aristotle, describing a person with *paideia* (the Greek anticipation of *humanitas*), speaks of one, 'who in his own person is able to judge critically in all or nearly all branches of knowledge and not merely in some special subject.'[7] The dominant Graeco–Roman model then was that of *humanitas*, and *theologia* was alongside or subordinate to *humanitas*. Man's knowledge of God or the gods was part of his wider knowledge of humanity and nature.

(f) Summary. To summarise this speedy review of the evolution of the Greek word *theologia*, it was seen. to relate to the gods or God; it was seen as a generic term with divisions into mythical, rational, and civil theology; stress was laid upon the philosophical, indeed metaphysical, dimension of theology; and theology was seen as a complementary part of a wider educational enterprise centred upon *humanitas*. Our tentative conclusions at this point are five. Firstly, that theology must relate to the gods or God. Insofar as it ceases to do so the question must be raised as to whether such reflection can retain the name 'theology'. As we have indicated, in practice the term mythology has been given to the stories of the gods in different religions and as a discipline

mythology has become separated from theology. Secondly, insofar as *theologia* was a term adapted by rather than coined by Christians, in principle the term cannot be confined to Christian theology as so often happens in modern writing. Wherever there are formulations of views about transcendent Reality in different traditions, there in principle we have *theologia.* Whether we think in terms of multiple theologies—Hindu, Buddhist, Christian, Muslim, Jewish, etc.—in dialogue, or in terms of a universal theology of religion within which there are universal theological categories overarching the different theologies, or in terms of the universalising of a tradition's specific theological categories to include others, the time is passing or past when, in our global world, theology can be glibly equated with Christian theology. Thirdly, the question is raised as to whether, even within the *theologia* of a particular culture, theology need be confined to discourse about God in the narrow sense. Can it be a generic term including different branches of thought within its scope? Fourthly, as far as Athens is concerned, there is a stress upon philosophical theology which will pass into the western inheritance along with the different stream of thought emanating from Jerusalem. Finally, *theologia* is seen as part of a wider integral educational exercise encompassing not only God and the gods but also (more importantly) humanity and (less importantly) nature.

2. THE ABSENCE OF THE WORD 'THEOLOGIA' FROM THE BIBLE

(a) Septuagint and Old Testament. How then was the word *theologia* applied to the stream of thought emanating from Jerusalem? In order to consider this we must look at the Old Testament words for the gods or God and their translation into the Greek of the Septuagint. The Septuagint is unique in that it was the first translated scripture. Insofar as scriptures are often taken to be written in a sacred language, whether it be Sanskrit, Arabic, Hebrew, or Pali, the notion of translation from the sacred language into an inferior or distorting medium is normally repugnant. The unique situ-

ation of Dispersion Judaism called forth the unusual expedient of translation from the original sacred Hebrew into Greek. During this process the Hebrew words for God were translated into Greek. What then were these Hebrew words, and how were they translated?

In the Old Testament there are three main generic designations for God, namely *'el*, *'eloah*, and *'elohim*.[8] *'el* in particular is both a common noun and a proper name for a particularised god. The individual, personal name for the Hebrew God is Yahweh. In the Septuagint *'el*, *'eloah* and *'elohim* are usually translated as *theos*, Yahweh is usually translated as *kyrios*. Philo offers a link between the Old Testament idea of Yahweh and the Greek idea of God. For Philo, *ho theos* is used for the good Creator God, *ho kyrios* for the kingly lord of the world, and *theos* without the article for the Word which mediates creation and revelation. However, as far as the word *theos* itself is concerned, its general use is as a translation of the words *'el*, *'eloah*, and *'elohim* as well as in direct reference to the Greek gods and God.[9] We therefore have the situation whereby we now study not kyriology, nor Yahwehology, but theology with the etymological implications involved.

(b) New Testament. In fact, of course, the word *theologia* as opposed to the word *theos* is not used in the New Testament. We may suppose that the habit of using *theologia* in relation to the Roman ceremonial gods and rites was a deterrent in this respect. The word *theologia* is inherited by Christian theology in two ways. In the first place, the word *theos* is used for the Christian God and so the way was opened for the word *theologia* to be used for the Christian account of God. *Theos* is used of the one, living, true and personal God who is the creator and upholder of the world. This God is spirit, father, personal; he has numerous attributes such as eternity, wisdom, righteousness, love, etc. Christ is viewed as the Son of God, and in various key texts such as Romans 9:5, John 1:1,1:18, 5:20,20:28, Titus 2:13, Matthew 27:46 the question is raised as to whether he is God. The notion of the Trinity is there in germ.[10] In the second place, two of the three Stoic uses of the term *theologia* are rejected by implication. The New Testament is antipathetic to the mythical and civic branches

of theology mentioned by the Stoics. Indeed, the early Church looks upon other gods, and especially the gods of the mystery religions in their sacramental setting, as *daimon* or *diabolos* rather than *theos*.[11] The earlier view of theology that is not rejected by implication is the Greek philosophical view. The way was opened for Greek philosophical theology to be used as a conceptual framework for the gospel.[12] Conversely it is not until our own day that Roman Catholic theologians such as Panikkar have been willing to admit theologically that the sacraments as opposed to the philosophy of others might be their normal way to God.[13]

3. THE PATRISTIC USE OF 'THEOLOGIA'

(a) Background. The actual word *theologia* surfaces in Christian thinking during the patristic period. Before we look briefly at the different uses of the word in patristic thought, it is worth making the trite but important point that *theologia* now becomes virtually the monopoly of a religious community. With the rise of the Christian church a new phenomenon became apparent in religious history, namely the exclusivistic religious community. Signs of the burgeoning of this phenomenon had already been apparent in the synagogue and in the mystery cults that arose in the Middle East in the wake of Alexander the Great's epic journey between West and East. However it was the Church which provided the first large-scale example of an exclusive religious community, and as theology arose within the Church it became the property of that religious community. In other words, *theologia* was not the product of a general culture as had been the case with Greece, it was the product of a particular group within the whole community.

Before we analyse in detail the patristic uses of the word *theologia* it is worth making the further point that they developed within a specific milieu which was important for its interpretation. After the beginnings of the Church in the first century when the Old Testament was still the vital starting-point, Hellenism and the Roman Empire became partners in dialogue with the Church, and the Christian community came to maturity within a wider, complex culture. In other words the Christian notion of *theologia* and Christian *theologia* itself arose in the work of the Apologists partly in response to the pressure of the surrounding non-Christian culture. After A.D. 313, with the conversion of the Roman Empire, *theologia* developed further within the more homogeneous culture of an increasingly Christian empire. Now there was little dialogue with potential counter-cultures or counter-religions. Christian *theologia*—indeed Christian institutions, Christian administrative structures, and Christian thought forms—grew up in western Europe (in the aftermath of the Roman Empire) at a time when western Europe was cut off from the rest of the world. Christian *theologia* could define itself in isolation without stimulus from or opposition from alternative *theologias*.[14]

(b) General use. A study of Lampe's *A Patristic Greek Lexicon* reveals a number of patristic uses of the word *theologia*.[15] It was used occasionally to refer to the scriptures in themselves. As Hugo of St. Victor later succinctly put it, 'Theologia, id est divina scripture.'[16] It begins to be used in the titles of books, and as Gregory of Nazianzus so rightly puts it, it is 'difficult to study'![17] The men of the Bible now replace the Greek poets as models of theologians and in different contexts Moses and St. John become the archetypes of the theologian.

(c) Clement and Origen. There is no time to investigate the patristic use of *theologia* in detail. We will single out three usages that are of more than usual importance. In the first place Origen used the term *theologia* to refer to Christian understanding of God as distinguished from Christian faith. Origen and Clement of Alexandria adopted and christianised Greek philosophy as a tool for conceptualising *theologia*. Clement speaks of 'the philosophy which really is philosophy' as being identified with 'true *theologia*'.[18] Clement and Origen lived in the 'Greek' milieu of Alexandria. They sought to express *theologia* in the thought-forms of those around them, to unite revelation and reason, to unite scripture and philosophy. For them, theology was a synthesis of what we would call dogmatic theology and philosophy of religion. Indeed they can be seen as the initiators of Christian systematic

theology. Origen's distinction between Christian faith and *theologia* as Christian understanding of God is important. On occasions in Christian history, faith and theology have been identified; faith has been equated with belief.[19] Origen recognised that *theologia* is an important but second-order activity; he saw that theology is secondary to faith. He may have something to teach us here.

(d) Theology restricted to the doctrine of the Trinity. Our second patristic example gives to the term *theologia* a more limited and yet potentially perhaps a more weighty meaning. It was taken to refer to the doctrine of God in a narrow sense. As the christological and trinitarian dialogue developed, *theologia* became centred, in the struggle with the Arians, on knowledge of the Persons of the Trinity. For example, in Athanasius' *Oratio I contra Arianos*, 18, *theologia* came to have the semi-technical meaning of knowledge of God in himself as distinguished from *oikonomia* which related to what God did through creation and salvation.[20] In other words, *theologia* in this sense was limited to part of Christian doctrine and did not constitute the whole of Christian doctrine. Indeed, Augustine, and later Aquinas, used the term Christian doctrine or *sacra doctrina* to refer to all Christian knowledge of which *theologia* was a part. This stress upon the need for a correct doctrine of God over against the Arians constituted the extension of a tendency to stress doctrine that was already latently there. Although *theologia* was limited at first to the doctrine of the Trinity, insofar as it was now yoked with the concept of doctrine the potentiality was there for *theologia* to be extended to a consideration of *all* Christian doctrine.

(e) St. Augustine. The third patristic example, that of St. Augustine, made explicit a meaning of *theologia* that we have touched on before. He gave a critique of the Stoic threefold division of *theologia* into mythical, rational, and civic. He singled out the rational division as being the true one and accentuated the importance of doctrine at the expense of myth in Christian theology. However, Augustine also did more than this. Like the Greeks, St. Augustine felt that *theologia* and *humanitas* were complementary. However for Augustine the *humanitas* model that he had inherited (grammar, languages,

history, geography, astronomy, dialectic, mathematics, rhetoric, and the philosophy of Plato) was a preparation for *theologia* rather than the other way around. There is no disputing that the basic axis of his model has now changed: it is now God rather than humanity, it is *theologia* rather than *humanitas*.

(f) *Importance of doctrine*. The idea that *theologia* involves doctrinal belief assumed increasing importance. In either case, whether theology was restricted to *theologia* as doctrine of God, or was widened to include *oikonomia* and doctrines of salvation, the idea that theology had something to do with doctrine was becoming of increased significance. Orthodoxy was becoming defined in terms of doctrine and therefore by implication of theology. This has not happened in other religious traditions where practice, as formulated in the Jewish Torah or the Muslim Sharilah, remained prior to doctrine, or where a combination of philosophical sensitivity and religious pluralism steered Buddhists and Hindus away from an undue concern with doctrine or theology.[21] This does not mean that other religions have no doctrines and no theology; it does mean that they have not given them the same weight as has Christianity.

4. THE SCHOLASTIC USE OF 'THEOLOGIA'

(a) *Background*. The Scholastic thinkers further developed the meaning of *theologia* and prepared the way for the so-called Golden Age when Theology became the Queen of the Sciences. A new factor in the medieval situation was the rise of universities at Oxford, Paris, Bologna, etc. For better or worse, *theologia* was destined to become an academic discipline in addition to an ecclesiastical one. An old factor now became accentuated, namely the isolation and besieged nature of European society wherein the Church held a monopoly situation. *Theologia* was destined to be influenced by successive entries of a rediscovered Aristotle; it was not yet subject to the stimulus of non-western thought. In the twelfth century

Abelard applied the term *theologia* to the philosophical treatment of Christian doctrine. His method of reconciling opposite authorities according to his formula of *Sic et Non* enabled him to erect a new systematic theology with the aid of another instalment of Aristotelian discoveries. In the same twelfth century there appeared the most famous of all the *Summae*, the systematic groupings of the patristic authorities, namely the *Sententiarum Libri Quattuor* of Peter Lombard in 1148–51.[22] Lombard's collection of sources relied especially upon Augustine, Hilary of Poitiers, and St. John of Damascus, but it was important for the way in which he organised his themes under the four headings of the Trinity, providence, and evil; creation, sin, and grace; incarnation, redemption, virtues, and commandments; and the seven sacraments and the four last things. *Theologia* now became the academic study of scripture and the *Sentences*; theology was now the systematic presentation of Christian doctrine.

(b) Entry of Aristotle. The following century, the century of Aquinas, saw the rise of the new mendicant orders and the third entry of Aristotle whereby his metaphysics, psychology, and ethics, as well as his natural science, became known in the West. What attitude would Christian theology take towards the new philosophy? In the Islamic world Avicenna and Averroes had offered a brilliant presentation of Aristotle within Islam but they had been virtually ignored within mainstream Islam and relegated to the status of a peripheral philosophical sect.[23] In the Jewish world Maimonides had offered his own exposition of Aristotelian categories but they were not integrated into medieval Judaism, and Maimonides's reputation within his community rested upon his work on the Talmud rather than upon his philosophical contributions.[24] In the world of Indian religion, the Hindu Upanishads and the Abhidharma section of the Buddhist Pali Canon already contained philosophy within the scriptures themselves, and for this and other reasons philosophy and theology have been more integrally related within India.[25] In the West, the Latin Averroists uncritically accepted Aristotle; St. Bonaventure and the Franciscan Augustinians on the whole rejected him; St. Thomas Aquinas accepted Aristotle's philosophy where

it coalesced with Christian theology, and christianised it or rejected it wherein it did not, thereby effecting a synthesis between the two.

(c) Aquinas: relation of theology and philosophy. Aquinas's philosophy of being, borrowed from Aristotle, enabled him to distinguish between philosophy and theology.[26] According to him, philosophy operates within its own circle to answer questions about man and the world; theology operates within its own circle to explicate the mystery of God through scripture and the fathers. Philosophy of religion is the indispensable handmaid of theology, and yet there is a difference between the two. For theology, God is given; for philosophy of religion, God's existence is not given, it remains to be proved.[27] For Aquinas and the position he represents, philosophy of religion provides an area of agreement with other religions, and indeed a medieval trilogue involving Muslims, Jews, and Christians existed in this very field.[28] However the area of theology, with its stress upon particular scriptures and authorities, does not, for Aquinas, offer the same hope of agreement.

(d) Theology as Queen of the sciences. Aquinas's view of *theologia* however goes deeper and wider than this useful distinction between theology and philosophy. According to him, the laws of being apply to the realm of theology and supernature which are what they are because of their nature. Theology is speculative learning susceptible of rational organisation by the intellect and involves knowing the reality of things whether natural or supernatural. In short, natural and revealed theology are the climax of all that is; theology is the Queen of the Sciences, and theology itself is scientific.[29]

(e) Theology as an integral discipline. Aquinas also asserts the integral nature of all theology in the narrower (supernatural) sense of the word. Dogmatic, moral, spiritual, mystical, and canonical theology are not separate disciplines, they are the connecting spokes of the same discipline.

(f) Summary. With Aquinas we have a watershed in the development of the word *theologia*. From being non-existent in the New Testament, *theologia* is now the Queen of the Sciences.

What are the main features of the development of the word and concept of *theologia* to this time? In the first place, it is the product of a religious community, namely the Church, rather than the product of a culture as had been the case in Greece. However, the rise of the universities opened up the possibility that theology would become more than the mere concern of a religious community. Secondly, theology is linked with doctrine, especially the doctrine of God but also in the later developments with Christian doctrine in general. This was a different development from the original Greek one wherein mythological stories rather than doctrines had been central. Thirdly, there had been a sometimes uneasy, sometimes fruitful, relationship between theology and philosophy. In Greece philosophy had held the dominant position, in the Christian developments theology became the major partner. Nevertheless philosophy of religion was more important in Christianity than in Judaism or Islam, and less integral than in Hinduism. Fourthly, Christian theology inherited much of its content from Israel and much of its conceptual method from Greece. Athens and Jerusalem often stood in dialectical relationship within Christian theology. However, these two strands presented the possibility of continuing dialogue *within* Christianity. There was little awareness of any theology *outside* Christian theology. Jewish and Muslim theology, insofar as they were known at all, tended to be viewed as heretical forms of Christianity rather than as theological systems in their own right. Buddhist, Chinese, and Indian theology were virtually unknown within the besieged city that was medieval Europe. As Christian theology was the only option, it was assumed that theology equalled Christian theology. The two were equated. Fifthly, theology in Aquinas's sense of revealed theology was viewed as one discipline containing a number of branches, not as a number of separate disciplines hopefully connected across disciplinary boundaries. Sixthly, not only was theology seen as an integral discipline within itself, it was also viewed by Aquinas as being continuous, according to the laws of being, with other forms of knowledge and as being the highest form of knowledge. This supremacy of theology within the unity of all knowledge was only possible because Christian theology was conceptualised within the categories of Greek thought which viewed science as the deduction of the particular from the general rather than the investigation of the particular in order to discover general hypotheses and laws arising from observation. Centuries later John Locke was adumbrating the same notion, 'Theology, which, containing the knowledge of God and his creatures, our duty to him and our fellow-creatures, and a view of our present and future state, is the comprehension of all other knowledge, directed to its true end.'[30] However, it was in the time of that same John Locke that movements were taking place that were to give new meanings to the word theology. Indeed Locke was the philosopher *par excellence* of a new empiricism that heralded the rise of our modern scientific world.

5. THE MODERN USE OF THE WORD 'THEOLOGY'

(a) Background. There were important theological developments during the period of the Reformation and Counter-Reformation but they did not involve major changes in the meaning of theology itself. Within the Roman Catholic community traditional modes and conceptions of theology remained virtually intact until the Councils of our own day. As far as the Reformation was concerned, it was the authoritative source for theology rather than the nature of theology that was at issue. The Reformers went back behind the scholastics to the Bible as the record of God's revelation with its stress upon salvation by faith and the priesthood of all believers.[31] They distrusted what appeared to them to be an overdue reliance upon reason and philosophy, and represented in part a retreat from Athens in the direction of Jerusalem. This meant that they had a greater liking for systematic theology than for philosophy of religion. However they introduced no new deep conception of what theology basically is. Dramatic changes in the meaning of *theologia*, now expressed in vernacular translations and languages, had to await dynamic developments within the modern world itself.

What then are these major changes? It is clearly not possible nor desirable to do a swift panoramic survey of modern Christian theology in order to demonstrate these changes. My purpose has been not to give a history of Greek and Christian theology but to show how the meaning of the word itself has changed as it has developed. Within the limits of time and space still available the need for stringent selection is more necessary than ever, and some of our comment will necessarily be prescriptive as well as descriptive.

(b) 'Theology' in a world of plural religions. The first change has been a growing awareness that we live in a world where there are a number of separate religious traditions, each with its own theology, however defined. After Vasco da Gama's voyage around Africa, the realisation slowly dawned in Europe that there were other religious traditions in the world of which Europe had not been aware during her medieval isolation. Along with this discovery of new traditions, there was a growing awareness that the Jewish and Muslim traditions were not mere epiphenomena of Christianity but separate traditions in their own right with their own theology. It is during the present century and above all since the Second World War that the evidence for this has become overwhelming and its importance apparent. Once the existence of other traditions was recognised it was also recognised that in some sense they had a theology. By 1841 Elphinstone was able to write, of India, 'their theology, mythology, philosophy . . . are almost entirely of the Hindu family.'[32] Quite apart from the use of the word theology in regard to the other traditions, there was the theological fact that, however Christians regarded other traditions, Islam and Judaism had a structurally similar monotheistic theology, and the Hindus in their *bhakti* tradition had a theology of a personal God. The test case was Buddhism. Although early Buddhism had no concept of a personal God, only of the gods, it did have the categories of Nirvana and Dharma as theological equivalents.[33] And so theology, which had meant an account of the gods or of God for the Greeks, and an account of God for the Christians, now came to refer to an account of God (in the widest sense) in other religious traditions.

(c) Theology in a multi-religious situation. The theological impli-

cations of this are enormous. Members of different religious traditions are coming to realise that in addition to the theological work that must be done *within* their own traditions, there is an additional theological task to be accomplished in regard to other religions in the global city of which we are all part. The main theological consequences are as follows.

In the first place, it is scarcely valid in this new pluralistic theological situation unthinkingly to equate theology with Christian theology. In our world there is Christian theology, Hindu theology, Muslim theology, Jewish theology, Buddhist theology; there is not a generic unqualified theology except in defined circumstances. Some of us have what we hope may be creative ideas for the renewal of Christian theology, and for the renewal of theology. We must be clear that these two enterprises are not necessarily identical. To refer to theology in general when what we really mean is Christian theology is to insinuate that other religions have no theology of their own; it is to purvey a subtle sort of Christian imperialism.[34]

The second consequence is that we must determine our theological attitude towards the other religious traditions of the world. There are basically seven possibilities and we will examine them in more detail later. There is the exclusivistic option, one tradition is right and the others are wrong; there is the option of a discontinuity theology, that one tradition has revelation which is God's downward coming to man whereas other traditions have only religion which is man's upward groping for God; there is the option of a secularisation theology whereby one tradition is able to harness the process of secularisation whereas others are not; there is the fulfilment option whereby one tradition fulfils the others which have truth, spirituality and God but only in part; there is the universalisation option whereby one tradition widens its theological categories to transcend the concepts within which they are strait-jacketed in order to comprehend the unknown God who is working within other traditions; there is the dialogue option whereby one engages in dialogue with the theological position of others; and finally there is the option of relativism: cultural, epistemological, and teleological. The theological task of all traditions to determine their theological attitudes towards the others is no longer merely an optional extra, it is becoming crucial.

The third consequence is that the question arises as to whether it is possible to construct a theology of comparative religion to make sense theologically of the total world religious situation in which we find ourselves. Is it possible to construct universal theological categories that are Christian but are also more than Christian to conceptualise the new world theological becoming? This is virgin ground and the task has hardly begun.[35] As we shall see, much depends in what we mean by the word theology.

Fourthly, and in the view of this book most importantly, there is the challenge and opportunity for Christian theology to renew itself through its encounter with the other religions.

(d) 'Theology' in a world of plural disciplines. The second change in the meaning of the word theology in the modern world has been effected by the rise of a number of new academic fields that were not present in the Greek world or in the world of Aquinas. Aquinas was able to view natural and revealed theology as the climax of all that is because other spheres of knowledge such as ethics, natural science, psychology, and metaphysics fitted into his basically Greek theology/philosophical world view. At the same time as John Locke was conceptualising his philosophy of empiricism, Newton and others were inaugurating a scientific revolution based upon experiment and observation that was to bring into being the modern discipline of natural science, a field of study very different from the natural science of the Greeks.[36] The rise of the new natural science in the seventeenth century was the precursor of the rise of a number of autonomous disciplines, partly influenced by the scientific model. Pioneers such as von Ranke in history, Durkheim in sociology, Freud and Jung in psychology, Tylor and Frazer in anthropology, created new disciplines with their own methodologies and their own models of reality.[37] The claim was made that these disciplines were scientific and neutral. In practice they were sometimes ideological and reductionistic. The fact remains that they described the world in ways that were not theological. Knowledge was becoming fragmented into separate compartments

and disciplines, some of which encroached upon territory that had been thought to be the province of theology: for example scientists pronounced upon creation and evolution, and psychologists had views about the unconscious mind or soul. The all-encompassing nature of Thomist theology was now inoperative and the question arose as to what was the discipline of theology as distinct from the disciplines of psychology, sociology, history, anthropology, science, etc.? The nature of the development of modern philosophy prompted the further question, the long-standing one, of what was the relationship between theology and philosophy? *Theologia* was replaced by natural science as the Queen of the Sciences and found herself being relegated to the periphery of knowledge.

(e)   The use of the word 'theology' within particular religious traditions. The third change in the meaning of theology in the modern world arises when we examine what it means in the context of a particular tradition. Granted that a number of new disciplines have arisen in the modern world, to what extent should they be adapted and incorporated within the overall umbrella of theology within a particular tradition? Is theology an academic subject with branches, a generic word for inter-related disciplines, or is it merely one discipline among many others within a particular tradition? At one extreme, doing theology thoughtfully can be seen as like thoughtfully doing all sorts of things—it can be seen as a craft which co-ordinates the methods and materials of other disciplines such as philosophy, linguistics, the arts, psychology, sociology, anthropology, science, ethics, history, and futurology. At the other extreme, it can be seen as a self-contained and *sui generis* activity that is practisable only in its own terms and within its own parameters, and is rigidly separate from other disciplines. How then can we resolve the matter?

Just how complex the question is can be seen by studying the article on theology in Hastings ERE.[38] The writer suggests that theology contains a historical or phenomenological branch, and a normative branch. Within the so-called historical or phenomenological branch of theology there are ten sections, namely history of religions, comparative religion, psychology of religion, biblical linguistics, biblical criticism, biblical history, biblical theology, church history, the history of doctrine, and the history of creeds and confessions. Within the so-called normative branch of theology there are twelve sections, namely apologetics, Christian dogmatics, Christian ethics, homiletics, liturgics, catechetics, pastoral theology, ecclesiastical polity, and evangelistic theology. It was doubtless in reaction partly to this kind of view of theology that Barth and his followers restricted the subject matter of theology to the Word of God declared in Christ and witnessed to in the Bible. It seems to me at this point that we have reached a terminological impasse. The word theology is being pressed into service in so many different ways that it has become confusing and to use it without elaborate definition may even be counter-productive. What can be done to resolve the question?

6. POSSIBLE DIRECTIONS FOR THE FUTURE

It is of course premature to offer any sweeping suggestions on the basis of this one chapter. More evidence and discussion are still needed. However, it would appear to be in order, in view of our review of the development of the term *theologia*, to indicate some of the possible directions of future discussion. This discussion may well centre upon the meaning and context of *theologia*.

(a) The word 'theology' within different contexts. To take context first, the discussion as to what *theologia* is has taken place in three different contexts. The popularly and academically dominant one has been that of a particular religious tradition, usually Christianity, although recently the theology of other traditions has received some attention. Macquarrie writes, 'Theology may be defined as the study which, through participation in and reflection upon a religious faith, seeks to express the content of this faith in the clearest and most coherent language available.'[39] According to this view, *theologia* has to do with and arises out of the experience of a particular religious tradition. Theology is Christian, Jewish, Muslim, Hindu, or Buddhist theology.

The second context was the original one of Greece. In that situation *theologia* was not the sole prerogative of a religious community. It arose within a culture. To be a rounded person one needed philosophy/*theologia* (knowledge of God or the gods) as well as the more important *paideia/humanitas* (knowledge of literature and humanity) and the less important science (knowledge of nature). According to this view, *theologia* is not necessarily limited to a religious community. To be human, humanity needs an integral awareness of Transcendence, humankind and nature, and therefore a conceptual awareness of *theologia, humanitas*, and science. In the Graeco-Roman model *humanitas* took precedence, in the medieval western European model *theologia* was predominant, in the modern western model natural science has dominated. Nevertheless, all are necessary, and *theologia* is not necessarily limited to a religious community.

The third context is the global situation in which we now live. Our modern *ecumene* is far wider than the Greek one. It is wider not just in the sense that there is the increasing desire for the renewal of *theologia* and *humanitas* to repair the imbalance and crisis produced by the scientific revolution; it is wider also in the sense that the *theologia* needed is unlikely to be provided by any one religious tradition operating unilaterally. What is needed is a theology of religion (or comparative religion) that will do justice to our new global situation. It is clear that the *theologia* arising out of the first context, that of a particular religious tradition, will remain important into the foreseeable future. It is likely that the *theologia* demanded by the second context, that which is needed to complement *humanitas* and natural science, will become more important. It is equally likely that the *theologia* or religion arising out of the third context, that of our present global situation, will also become more important.[40] Although our main concern is with Christian theology, we recognise that in our modern multi-disciplinary and mutli-religious global context theology must both stress and transcend the Christian community.

(b)   The many different meanings of the word 'theology'. But is there a basic meaning of the word *theologia* that can be applied to

any context? As we have seen, in the process of its develop- ment the word has acquired a number of different meanings. For the Greeks, it meant talk of God or the gods; for the early medievals, it denoted the doctrine of the Trinity and, later, doctrine in a wider sense; for Aquinas *theologia* was the highest form of, and the fullest comprehension of, *all* knowledge; for some later Protestants it was a *sui generis* activity radically distinguished from other knowledge; for some recent thinkers, the *theologia* of a religion was seen to encompass not only its doctrine but also its communal structure, worship, ethics, social involvement, scripture, aesthetics and spirituality. Like the word 'religion' the word 'theology' has been used in radically different ways.

(c) Possible future uses of the word 'theology'. It is difficult, at this early stage to draw firm conclusions as to what *theologia* basically is. Tentatively, however, we offer the following suggestions. Firstly, *theologia* has always had to do with God or Transcendence. A theology of communism, humanism or other Transcendence-querying phenomena would therefore be difficult to conceptualise. Secondly, *theologia* has usually been a second-order activity arising out of faith rather than being equated with faith. Thirdly, *theologia* has usually taken a doctrinal form involving the use of words, sentences, and concepts.

Whatever, then, *theologia* is not (and we are not yet ready to abandon the other meanings of the word without further research), it *is* in the first place conceptual assertions primarily about God or Transcendence, but also about other doctrines, in *particular* religious traditions; in the second place it is in general our conceptualisation of God or Transcendence (whereas *humanitas* is our conceptualisation of man, and natural science is our conceptualisation of nature); and in the third place it is global humanity's attempt to make sense of human kind's global experience of Transcendence.

Christian theology is therefore conceptual assertions primarily about God as mediated through Christ (i.e. the Trinity and Christology), but also about other doctrines; it is part of a wider enterprise (confusingly also called Christian theology but perhaps better termed Divinity or Christian studies) that deals with Christian community, worship, social involvement, ethics, scripture, aesthetics and spirituality; it is closely connected with these seven other elements within Christian studies, especially spirituality, as it reflects upon Christian faith; and as it renews itself by dialogue with other religions it stands alongside the humanities and the natural sciences in the conceptualising of a new global world.

FOOTNOTES

1. The substance of part of this chapter was delivered at Harvard University in June 1979 at a conference in honour of Professor Wilfred Cantwell Smith. Smith analysed the word 'religion' in: W C Smith *The Meaning and End of Religion* (Macmillan, New York, 1963).

2. H G Liddell and R Scott (eds), *A Greek-English Lexicon*, pp 791–2 (Clarendon, Oxford, 1940). On the early history and meaning of *theologia*, see Werner Jaeger, *The Theology of the Early Greek Philosophers*, pp 1–10 (Oxford, 1947).

3. See J Murray (ed), *A New English Dictionary*, p 275 (Clarendon, Oxford, 1919).

4. See *New Catholic Encyclopaedia*, vol vi, pp 745–7 (McGraw-Hill, New York, 1967).

5. See *New Catholic Encyclopaedia* vol x, pp 334–5.

6. See Aulus Gellius' *Noctes Atticae* 13.16, quoted by Otto Bird *Cultures in Conflict*, pp 14–15 (University of Notre Dame Press, Notre Dame, Indiana, 1976).

7. Aristotle *Parts of Animals* I.i.639a 1–12, quoted by Otto Bird, op. cit., pp 12–13. For Greek *Paideia*, see Werner Jaeger, *Paideia: The Ideals of Greek Culture*, vols. 1, 2 3 (tr. by G. Highet) (Oxford Univ. Press, New York, 1939) 43, 44 and W Jaeger, *Humanism and Theology* (Marquette University Press, Milwaukee, 1943).

8. J Hastings (ed), *Encyclopaedia of Religion and Ethics*, vol vi, pp 253–4 (T&T Clark, Edinburgh, 1913).

9. G Kittel (ed), *Theological Dictionary of the New Testament*, vol iii, pp 79–101 (Eerdmans, Grand Rapids, Michigan, 1964).

10. *The Interpreter's Dictionary of the Bible* (Abingdon, Nashville, 1962), pp 430–6.

11. See G Kittel, op. cit., vol ii, pp 16–19, 79–81.

12. See *New Catholic Encyclopaedia* on Justin Martyr (vol viii, pp 94–5). Also Werner Jaeger, *Early Christianity and Greek Paideia* (Harvard University Press, Cambridge, 1961).

13. See R Panikkar on 'Christianity and World Religions' in *Christianity* (Punjabi University, Patiala, 1969).

14. This did not preclude theological disagreement *within* the Christian tradition.

15. G W H Lampe (ed), *A Patristic Greek Lexicon*, pp 627–8 (Clarendon, Oxford, 1961).

16. See J Murray, op. cit., p 275.

17. G W H Lampe, op. cit., p 268.

18. See *New Catholic Encyclopaedia* on Clement (vol iii, pp 943–4); on Origen (vol x, pp 767–74).

19. See W C Smith *Belief and History* (University Press of Virginia, Charlottesville, 1977).

20. G W H Lampe, op. cit., pp 940–3.

21. The lack of a central body within the Hindu and Buddhist traditions is another relevant factor.

22. See *New Catholic Encyclopaedia*, vol xii, pp 94–6.

23. See W M Watt *Islamic Philosophy and Theology* (Edinburgh University Press, 1962).

24. J Sarachek *Faith and Reason: the Conflict over the rationalism of Maimonides* (reprint New York, 1970 (1935).

25. The great Hindu *aeharyas* were essentially exegetists of sacred books which were, in the case of *Vedanta*: the *Upanishads*, the *Bhagavad Gita*, and the *Vedanta Sutras*.

26. See *New Catholic Encyclopaedia*, vol xiv, p 52.

27. Ibid., p 52.

28. Aquinas built upon the work of Avicenna, Averroes, and Maimonides.

29. See V J Bourke *Aquinas's Search for Wisdom* (Milwaukee, 1965).

30. See J Murray op. cit., p 275.

31. See for example O Chadwick *The Reformation* (Penguin, 1964). A more detailed account is given in Wolfhart Pannenberg, *Theology and the Philosophy of Science*, pp 228–296 (Westminster Press, Philadelphia, 1976).

32. See J Murray, op. cit., p 275.

33. *Nirvana* is described in absolute terms and the *Dharma* is taken to be pre-existent and eternal.

34. The same applies to the use of the word 'philosophy' when what is meant is 'western philosophy'.

35. The work of Wilfred Cantwell Smith remains one of the most promising forays into this area, e.g., *Toward a World Theology* (Westminster Press, Philadelphia, 1981).

36. See H Butterfield *Origins of Modern Science* (Bell & Sons, London, 1949).

37. As applied to religion see J Waardenburg *Classical Approaches to the Study of Religion*, vol i (Mouton, The Hague, 1973).

38. J Hastings, op. cit., vol xii, pp 297–9.

39. J Macquarrie *Principles of Christian Theology*, p 1 (Scribners, New York, 1966).

CHAPTER FOUR

CHRISTIAN THEOLOGICAL ATTITUDES TO OTHER RELIGIONS

I. INTRODUCTION

Keeping in view our discussion of what Christian theology basically is, it is now our task to analyse the various Christian theological attitudes to other religious traditions. I use the word 'attitudes' advisedly, because, as we shall see, there are many possible theological attitudes that Christians can adopt towards others. Although for some Christians one particular theological attitude is 'correct', there is no general consensus throughout the worldwide Christian community whereby all Christians are agreed upon the obvious superiority or validity of such a single theological attitude. In this chapter I shall therefore sum up the various possible Christian theological attitudes that are available to the Christian who wishes to reflect theologically upon the multi-religious situation of our contemporary world.

It is not our aim to give a history of Christian theological attitudes to others. I hope to accomplish this in another volume. However it is a truism to say that there has been a greater urgency for reflection upon this matter when Christians have been in existential contact with other religions. It was a live issue in the life of the early church as she attempted to situate herself in a world which contained Jews, Mystery Religions, and a plethora of other religious groups. It has been an increasingly urgent matter since western Europe and therefore western Christians, in the persons of early world navigators such as Vasco da Gama, discovered eastern religious traditions that had been virtually unknown in medieval Europe. These traditions were later given by westerners the names of Hinduism, Buddhism, Zoroastrianism, Shintoism, Taoism, and so on. As Wilfred Cantwell Smith has pointed out these very names represented an implicit desire by westerners to classify other religious traditions in western terms rather than in their own terms, and as Edward Said has pointed out Orientalists in general have been tempted to classify the Orient according to western rather than oriental interests. The point is that, however they were classified, and however they were named, other religious traditions were now known to exist. What theological attitude should Christians adopt towards them? Finally in our own century, and above all since the Second World War, an awareness of other religious traditions has become unavoidable and this has given a further stimulus to Christian theological attempts to define an attitude towards them.

In this chapter, we are concerned with *Christian* theological attitudes towards *other* religions. This way of setting up the problem involves three important pre-suppositions. First it is assumed that the theological attitudes concerned are adopted by Christian theologians looking out from within the Christian community upon others who are non-Christians. To a greater or lesser extent the mentality involved is that of a 'we' who are Christians and that of a 'they' who are non-Christians. This designation is not necessarily self-obvious. Indeed one of the most revealing things about any intellectual stance is the meaning within that stance of that small word 'we'. Does it refer to my family, my town, my state, my civilisation, my trade, my religious tradition, my globe, or what? Is the 'we' involved limiting or all-embracing? This is a moot point. Indeed if we are to think globally it might be argued, as we shall see in the next chapter, that the 'we' involved should be all humankind. As far as the present discussion is concerned the 'we' involved is the Christian tradition *not* the human race. However the Christian tradition concerned is the *whole* Christian tradition not any particular part of it. The time is passing if not past when an analysis of Christian theological attitudes to other religions can be pursued in denominational terms.

Second there is the corollary that the 'others' are to some extent other. There may be theological overlaps, meaningful dialogue, and global co-operation between Christianity and other religions but the fact remains that the Christian tradition and other traditions are separate. By the same token it is quite possible for other religious traditions to form their *own* theological attitudes towards other religions including Christianity. It would then be the case that Islam say could adopt certain theological attitudes in respect of other religions, and those other religions would include Christianity.

Third our concern is with Christian *theological* attitudes. We have indicated in the last chapter our view of what Christian theology is. We have suggested that there are eight elements in Christian Studies: the Christian community, Christian rituals, Christian ethics, Christian social and political involvement, Christian scripture, Christian concepts, Christian aesthetics, and Christian spirituality. The main concern of Christian theology is with Christian concepts (and to a lesser extent Christian spirituality), and with the God and Christ to whom they point. Therefore, while it is urgent that Christians and their fellows from other religions should co-operate in good works such as digging wells together in places of need, this concern belongs more properly to Christian ethics than to Christian theology as such. We will concentrate upon the more properly theological concerns of Christian attitudes to other religious traditions.

2. CHRISTIAN ATTITUDES TO OTHER RELIGIOUS TRADITIONS

(a) Exclusivism. The first possible attitude is that of exclusivism. In its absolute form this viewpoint would state that other religions have no God or spirituality, their followers are pagans doomed to go to hell, and no compromise is possible with them. Exclusivism can take two main forms. On the one hand, it can take an institutional form and this would be found classically in the Roman Catholic dogma *Extra ecclesiam nulla salus* (outside the Church there is no salvation).[3] On the other hand, it can take a doctrinal form whereby salvation is defined in terms of true doctrine. This approach would be typified in the Fundamentals of 1912–14 with their stress

upon the inerrancy of the Bible, the Second Coming and Final Judgment, the deity and infallible power of Christ, His sacrificial atonement and penal substitution, and the supernatural acts of God seen especially in the Virgin Birth, miracles, and resurrection of Christ.[4] Implicit in the exclusivist position is the notion that salvation is restricted to Christians, and other traditions are excluded from the realm of salvation.

Because of its starkness, the exclusivist position has rarely been held in its absolute form. Approximations to it were present in the early Christian attitude towards the mystery religions, the work of Tertullian, Christian theological views at the time of the Crusades, and some Protestant views during the heyday of the British Empire. More often there has been exclusive opposition to some aspects of other religions as being false and wrong together with the admission that in limited ways other aspects of those same religions might contain glimpses of the truth. An obvious example of this is the past Christian theological opposition to the rituals and sacraments of other religions allied to an occasional willingness to admit that the philosophy or ethics of others might have some validity. Thus the Old Testament condemned idolatry on the part of other religions but was able to assimilate ideas from Persia; the early church condemned food offered to idols and polytheism as the work of demons but saw Greek philosophy and Jewish law as schoolmasters to bring Greeks and Jews to Christ; the early modern Roman Catholic missionaries to India and China had problems with the rituals and sacraments of the Hindus and Chinese but found elements of value in aspects of Indian philosophy and Confucian ethics. It is only in our own day, in the work of Roman Catholic scholars such as Panikkar that Christians have been willing to admit that the *sacraments* of others might be their normal way to God.

However in general the exclusivist position has been one of watertight opposition to other religious traditions. The Christian tradition, its institutions and/or doctrines, was exclusively right; other religions were exclusively wrong. The ark of salvation was to be found within the Christian sphere; outside the Christian milieu was no salvation.

The merit of exclusivism in some Christian eyes is its simplicity. The demerit is its starkness and insensitivity to others. Since the Vatican Councils of our own day, and indeed since before them, the exclusiveness of *Extra ecclesiam nulla salus* has been modified. Protestants who may have been attracted by the theological neatness of doctrinal exclusivism have found their own Christian ethics taking them in another direction with its moral imperative to love one's neighbour. A growing awareness of those of other religions has shown that they too have their saints, and that the monotheistic traditions share a high view of God as creator, as personal, and as transcendent. How can they therefore be exclusively wrong?

(b) Discontinuity. The second option is that of discontinuity. According to this position, there is a discontinuity between God's downward coming to humanity in the person of Jesus Christ, and humanity's upward groping for God on the part of the religious traditions. In other words, there is a discontinuity between 'revelation' which is seen according to this school of thought as God's revealing himself to human beings in the form of Jesus Christ, and 'religion' which is seen according to this school of thought as a human attempt on the part of the religions of this world to reach upward to try and find out God. The two movements, God's downward revelation and humanity's upward groping—do not meet. There is discontinuity between them.

While it is held by those who espouse this theological viewpoint that religion (humanity's own seeking for God) is often present within the Christian tradition, it is clear that insofar as revelation hinges upon Jesus Christ as the revealed Word of God it is within the Christian tradition that revelation so understood is going to be found. By implication other religions are not within the sphere of revelation.

The discontinuity approach is seen most clearly in the work of Karl Barth and Hendrik Kraemer. As Barth uncompromisingly puts it:[5]

Revelation does not link up with a human religion which is already present and practised. It contradicts it, just as religion previously contradicted revelation. It displaces it, just as religion previously displaced revelation; just as faith cannot link up with a mistaken faith, but must contradict and displace it as unbelief, as an act of contradiction.

On the face of it, this is merely another form of exclusivism. However it is not quite as simple as that. In other places Barth is not so uncompromising in his view of religion. Moreover, he knew very little about other religions. He was not analysing theologically the Christian attitude to other religions. He was speaking to a historical situation within Protestant theology whereby liberal Protestant theologians ranging from Schleiermacher to Troeltsch had placed the concept of religion at the heart of theology. He was taking part therefore in an internal wrangle within Protestant theology rather than addressing directly the theological question of the Christian approach to other religious traditions.

Barth's follower Hendrik Kraemer did have first-hand knowledge of other religions, especially Islam, and we see the discontinuity approach more clearly in his work. By contrast with Barth's writings, notably his massive *Church Dogmatics*, which spoke to a western European situation, Kraemer's *The Christian Message in a Non-Christian World* was written for the Tambaram conference in India in 1938 and it spoke more directly to the question of the other religions.

Kraemer made the point that each religion revolves around its own axis and must be seen as a whole. He states:[6]

> Every religion is a living, indivisible unity. Every part of it—a dogma, a rite, a myth, an institution, a cult—is so vitally related to the whole that it can never be understood in its real function, significance and tendency, as these occur in the reality of life, without keeping constantly in mind the vast and living unity of existential apprehension in which this part moves and has its being.

Kraemer's notion of the wholeness of different religions bears some similarity to my own model outlined in an earlier chapter. I also see each religious tradition as a mesh of eight interlinked elements which connect together to make up a total tradition. The difference is that in my model each religious tradition is not so rigid. Each tradition contains a congeries of views and elements that together make up the whole. There is no such thing as a monolithic Christianity, as this very chapter demonstrates. The Christian tradition can contain within itself seven different approaches to other religions and still remain the Christian tradition. Moreover in my model the differences between religious traditions are not so rigid. Insofar as all traditions contain the eight inter-linked elements we described earlier, this sets up the possi-bility of comparison between these elements in a way that will not necessarily do violence to the wholeness of each tradition. In addition to this, world events since the Second World War have conspired to throw traditions more closely together so that it is more possible for a Christian (while remaining a Christian) to participate in another tradition. A Martin Luther King, for example, can gain inspiration from the work of a Hindu, Mahatma Gandhi, in order to pursue his Christian goals.

However Kraemer's closeness to the non-European situ-ation of the church made him more ready than Barth both to analyse other religions, and to grapple with their value. 'To become more deeply aware of the stupendous richness and depth of religious life in *all* religions has made the ques-tion of value and truth in the non-Christian religions more, not less, acute',[7] he states. Nevertheless at the end of the day he developed a discontinuity approach. In spite of his attempts to avoid explicit condemnation of other reli-gions—and it is this fact that makes the discontinuity approach different from the exclusivistic approach—Kraemer maintains the discontinuity between 'revelation' and 'religion'. As he puts it:[8]

> Christianity as a phenomenon in history has to be considered as *a* form of religion just like the others, although, also like them, it has, of course its peculiar emphases and concerns. This thesis must constantly be repeated in order to avoid the frequently occurring iden-tification or partial identification of Christianity, one of the religions, with the Revelation of God in Christ.

To reinforce Kraemer's point let us quote him again:[9]

> In the illuminating light of the revelation in Christ, which lays bare the moving and grand but at the same time *distressing and desperate reality* of human religious life as reflected in the various religions, all 'similarities' and points of contact become dissimilarities.

Kraemer's position resembles the dialectical theology of Emil Brunner who was able to assert, 'Jesus Christ is both the Fulfilment of all religion and the Judgment on all religion'.[10] Their vision of religion is wider than that of Barth in that they can see Christ as in some sense fulfilling religion but it is also negative in that they see Christ as judging the distortions in other religions. True fulfilment is therefore not possible because any continuity between the Christian tradition and other traditions is offset by the judgmental revelation found in what Kraemer calls 'biblical realism'.

Kraemer's position, modified in *Religion and the Christian Faith* (1956) and *World Cultures and World Religions* (1960), set the agenda for discussion of Christian theological attitudes to others in the pre- and post-war years. Its biblical realism and clear-cut distinction between revelation and religion appealed to some. To others it appeared to give only part of the biblical witness, it failed to see that other religions (for example Islam with its stress upon the Koran as the Word of God) gave an equal stress to revelation, and it applied an abstract western theological viewpoint to obstinately non-western situations. In terms of my own model, it undervalued the transcendent reality, the mediating focus, and the faith that other religions felt they possessed.

(c) Secularisation. The third attitude is that of secularisation theology. It is less overtly theological than the first two in that it emphasises movements in the secular world as being vital for forming a realistic Christian theological attitude to other religions. However in spite of the sociological assumptions underpinning it, secularisation theology has developed a viable theological attitude to the other religious traditions of the world.

A powerful statement of this option appeared in Arend van Leeuwen's *Christianity in World History*. His thesis was that the modern process of secularisation was a God-given gift to the world and that it was, in effect, an agent of the Gospel. The secularisation process was the outworking of the rise of modern science and technology. Modern science and technology had arisen in the West, and it seemed to van Leeuwen that there was a good reason for this. Indeed he posed the question as to why modern science had not emerged in other civilisations such as those of China, India, or the Middle East. He gave the answer that those civilisations did not possess the necessary conceptual roots to allow of the appearance of modern science or technology. The western world on the other hand did possess the indispensable roots of the Judaeo–Christian theological tradition. As van Leeuwen puts it, the process of secularisation 'cannot be rightly and properly weighed unless one realises that the vital impulse behind it comes from the biblical message and that the course it has taken has its beginning in biblical history'.[11] God created the world out of nothing. It was not doomed to go on in cycles for ever. It had a beginning and it would have an end. God revealed himself through the prophets and He became incarnate in the world in Jesus Christ. This world and the welfare of the people in it were therefore important. History had a purpose. It was moving towards an appointed end. Progress, however defined, was meaningful. Matter and the body were not illusory but real. For God not only created the world, He also created humanity in his own image and gave humanity dominion over the world. It was therefore the prerogative of humankind to subdue the earth. It was humanity's duty under God to develop the earth which was separate from the people who lived on it just as those people were separate from the God who created them.

According to van Leeuwen it is these theological roots of the Judaeo–Christian tradition that paved the way for modern science and technology to develop. Out of them arose the process of secularisation so that 'Christianisation and secularisation are thus involved together in a dialectical relation'.[12] Accordingly secularisation is the fruit of the Christian Gospel. It enables humanity to achieve liberation from the ancient fetters of religious bondage, injustice, fate, sacred rulers, cosmic powers, and those forces that prevent the human race from attaining its true destiny under God. Insofar as Christianity provided the theological seedbed for secularisation to emerge, it can cope with that process and help it to develop.

The other religions, by contrast, are seen by van Leeuwen to be 'ontocratic'. Their myths and world views, until recently, bound them in a sacred world that was ontocratic and did not allow them to distinguish sufficiently between nature, humanity and God. It was impossible, therefore, for them to produce modern science and technology because they were not able to distance themselves from nature in order to investigate it. They were also threatened by the process of secularisation which they did not produce and which they found difficult to handle. At worst they would wither away before the process of secularisation; at best they would endure a traumatic experience in coping with it.

The type of secularisation theology used by van Leeuwen has been pursued in various directions by Bonhoeffer, Harvey Cox, van Buren and others. The disquiet they showed towards 'religion' was the extension in a secular direction of the same disquiet shown by Barth and Kraemer, and it was an attempt to take the technological urban world of industry and cybernetics seriously. It promoted new thinking about the need to liberate humanity from injustice, oppression, poverty, fate, the social pressures of traditional societies, and the chains of cosmic powers. There are echoes of later liberation theology in van Leeuwen's statement:[13]

> The best guarantee of real 'religious liberty' is in the readiness of Christians to make common cause with all those movements and individuals who wish to promote liberty as such—liberation, that is to say, from the fetters of 'sacred' tradition, together with the renewal of society in the direction of a truly secular and man-made order of life.

Implied here is the presupposition that Christians are in the vanguard of the secularisation process which is bringing a new freedom, justice and fulfilment to humanity whereas other religions are wedded to sacred world views that inhibit them from advancing naturally into the new freedom, justice and fulfilment which form the birthright of humankind.

We have spent time on this viewpoint because variants of it have been influential in the background thinking of liberation theology and of important elements in the World Council of Churches today, and because they presuppose a condescending view of other religions as ontocratic and outmoded.

Secularisation theology is valuable in that it brings out the link between the rise of modern science, technology and secularisation and the theological roots of the Judaeo–Christian tradition. It has promoted clearer thinking about the need to take seriously our modern urban technological society as being within the providence of God. It has stressed the importance of a new freedom and justice for human beings around the world.

However, it also ascribes a too-sacred and too-liberating role to science and technology. Since van Leeuwen wrote in 1964 it has become clear that, while science has been helpful in regard to some problems, it has helped to engender others such as the ecological crisis, pollution hazards, population growth, and the threat of nuclear war. It is no longer clear that the solution to the problems produced by science and technology lies in science and technology. As Laszlo puts it, 'the root causes even of physical and ecological problems are the inner constraints on our vision and values'.[14] Lying behind our vision and values are complex factors including, as we now realise, transcendent and spiritual dimensions.

Secularisation theology also too glibly equates secularisation, westernisation and Christianisation. Other cultures may engage in the secularisation process but they can do it in their own way. Muslim cultures can secularise in a Muslim way, Buddhist cultures in a Buddhist way, Jewish culture in a Jewish way, and so on. Secularisation need not be equated with westernisation, nor need secularisation be equated with Christianisation. The whiff of imperialism lies behind these equations.

Moreover secularisation, unguardedly fostered, builds up a momentum of its own that may transform it into secularism. The Judaeo–Christian tradition brings with it the tradition of prophecy and the feeling is growing that the secularisation process calls for prophetic judgment as well as enthusiastic blessing.

It is interesting that Harvey Cox, whose book *Secular City* was an influential counterpart to the work of van Leeuwen, has now become apprised of eastern religions in his later work.[15] Eastern spiritual leaders are pointing out that the world needs spiritualisation as well as secularisation. I have shown elsewhere that the hierarchy and autonomy between God, humanity, and nature registered by the Judaeo–Christian tradition have become magnified into a split of consciousness between the material, humane, and transcendent elements within western humanity's consciousness, and into a split between the natural sciences, the humanities, and religious studies in western education that are unhelpful. We need a reintegration of these splintered elements that, while garnering the fruit of the secularisation process, will bring together again what has unwittingly been put asunder. In achieving this, the other world religions, which are making their own adaptation to the process of secularisation, will be of great help.

(d) Fulfilment. Fulfilment theology has a venerable history in Christian thought. Fulfilment theologians, from Clement of Alexandria to the present day, have pointed out that God has not left himself without a witness in the other religious traditions. Other religions do have God, they do have spirituality, they do have truth, but they have them in part rather than in wholeness. They are destined to be fulfilled by Christ.

Fulfilment theology has taken many forms. One form centres around the problematic notion of an essence of religion. If it can be shown that there is an essence of religion, it can also be shown that although all religions partake of that essence the Christian tradition partakes of it more fully than the others. For Lord Herbert of Cherbury, the essence of religion lay in the five common notions he felt lay behind all religions: the fact of a supreme God, the need to worship God, the connection of virtue with piety, the need for repentance, and the fact of reward or punishment after death; for Kant it was the moral imperative; for Schleiermacher it was the feeling of absolute dependence; for Otto it was a numinous sense of the holy; for Farmer it was the personal encounter with God; for Eliade it was the sacred manifested through symbols and hierophanies.[16] All religions are taken to contain and manifest the essence of religion, whatever that might be, but the Christian tradition does it more fully than the others. For example in Eliade's thought all religions share the symbols of the sacred tree and holy water as manifestations of the sacred but in the cross and baptism there are supreme examples of those two symbols.

There are problems in thinking in terms of essences. Is there such a thing as an essence of religion, or an essence of Christianity? Essences, by definition, don't change but religious traditions visibly do change. Moreover if there is such a thing as the essence of religion how can it be seen better or more fully in one tradition than another? Nevertheless phenomenologically fulfilment of the essence of religion in the first species of fulfilment theology.

The second is the fulfilment of other religious traditions. This can take an active form: Christ fulfilled the law and the prophets of Israel, and Christ fulfilled the philosophy of Greece. In practice, this fulfilment was only a partial accomplishment. The Jews within the Jewish tradition do not, of course, admit that Christ fulfilled the law and the prophets, nor do modern-day humanists admit that Christ fulfilled the philosophy of Greece. They would be inclined to claim that privilege for themselves. However it is clear that the Christian tradition did in fact, if only in part, fulfil the law and the prophets insofar as the Christian scripture includes both the Old and New Testaments. It is also clear that Christian theology made liberal use of Greek philosophical concepts in its task of interpreting Christ. In modern times, as we shall see later, it is also the case that the Christian tradition is fulfilling primal religion in places such as Africa where in African Christianity the traditional African concepts of a High God and intermediary deities, ancestors, or spirits are fulfilled by the Christian God mediated by Christ.

In general, however, fulfilment theology is more static. It is the theological assertion that other religions do possess God, spirituality and truth and that they are fulfilled conceptually by Christ rather than by the practical outcome of hordes of people actually becoming Christians. Often lying behind fulfilment theology there is a Logos doctrine. There is the notion that all people partake in the Logos through creation, that the cosmic Christ informs all persons, that God is at work in other religions, that their own spirituality is real, but that in principle they are fulfilled by the perfect Logos who is Christ.

An important early modern example of fulfilment theology was J N Farquhar who wrote *The Crown of Hinduism* in 1913. Farquhar was different from the exclusivistic style of theologians who had preceded him in India. His Christian commitment was clear, but he had a real sympathy for India and for the Hindu tradition and he had a moving concern for accurate scholarship about Indian religions. His basic thesis was that the Hindu tradition contained good features that needed to be understood rather than condemned by Christians but that Jesus Christ is the fulfilment or the 'crown' of Hinduism for it is in Him that the authentic desires, quests, aspirations and longings of the Hindu find their completion, their fulfilment, and their crown. 'Not in arrogance, not in partisanship, do we say this', he wrote, 'but with wide open eyes and with full consciousness of the stupendous character of the claim we make'.[17]

Another example of fulfilment theology is the late R C Zaehner. The two phases of his fulfilment thought illustrate the static fulfilment thought we are discussing now and the notion of the dynamic fulfilment of the cosmic process by Christ we will discuss later. Like Farquhar, Zaehner was an amateur (rather than trained) theologian, he had a deep interest in Indian religion, and he was a committed Christian. Like Farquhar too part of his work, notably his volumes on Zoroastrianism and Hinduism, involved the sympathetic description of other religious traditions. In addition to being an expert in comparative religion, he was at heart a fulfilment theologian and he saw Christ fulfilling all the religious traditions of humankind. 'Unless I am greatly mistaken', he wrote, 'all the strands we have been trying to bring together in the different religions, meet only in one place, and that is in the religion of Jesus Christ, for Christ indeed comes to fulfil not only the law and the prophets of Israel, but also the "law and prophet" of the Aryan race'.[18] Accordingly Christ was 'the true Tao',[19] 'the true answer to Job,[20] and 'the fulfilment of the hope of Yudhisthira';[21] the Gospel was the 'fertilisation of Nirvana';[22] Rama and Krishna 'both in their way prefigure Christ';[23] and 'to be a Christian, you must be both a Marxist and a Buddhist, both Confucian and Taoist, for in Christ all that has abiding value meets'.[24] One by one, Zaehner takes up various concepts from different religions and shows how they are fulfilled in Christ: incarnation (the Hindu deities Rama and Krishna, and the Buddhist Bodhisattvas), saintliness and morality (the Hindu hero Yudhisthira), humility (Taoism), mysticism (the Indian religious pole), suffering (Job), dying to self (the Buddha), resurrection (Zoroaster), and the prophetic religious pole (Israel). At this point Zaehner was a static fulfilment theologian. His view of fulfilment was theoretical and conceptual rather than dynamic.

In his later work, Zaehner was captivated by the thought of Teilhard de Chardin and he became an intellectual disciple of Teilhard's. He now recast his fulfilment theology into a dynamic mould so that he saw Christ as fulfilling the whole cosmic process, and in this of course he was following the path mapped out by Teilhard. This third kind of fulfilment theology is fulfilment of process. It had been anticipated to some extent in Hegel's dialectics, but it is brought out more deeply in the later Zaehner's interpretation of Teilhard.

Zaehner took up Teilhard's notion of creative evolution whereby the world had evolved in stages punctuated by genetic leaps from the simple cell, to plant life, to animal life, and finally to human life. This creative evolution was still continuing and had its focus in humanity. The mass of the human race was still evolving and its point of convergence, its goal of fulfilment, was Omega Point or the Cosmic Christ. The other world religions were involved in this creative evolution and they would find their true fulfilment along with the rest of humanity when their treasures were taken up into the Cosmic Christ. It is clear at this point that Christ is no longer merely the static fulfilment of the world's religious traditions, He is the goal of the whole cosmic process, natural and human, religious and non-religious. He is the crown of the cosmic process itself.

Fulfilment theology is an honourable attempt to combine respect for other religions with a sense of the unique fullness of Christ. However other religions can have their own fulfilment theology. Sri Aurobindo sees the world religious process converging on Mother India rather than the Cosmic Christ, and Sir Muhammad Iqbal sees it converging upon a kind of ideal Islam.[28] In any case, evolutionary theories in general are not as attractive as they once were. At the level of fulfilment of essence or static fulfilment of traditions, a Hindu such as Radhakrishnan will say that Advaita Vedanta, the ultimate realisation that we are one with the Godhead, is a more fulfilled form of religion than is found in Christianity; Muslims will say that the Koran fulfils the Bible. Moreover all religious traditions are very complex and to posit a monolithic fulfilment of one by another, either actively or statically, is usually to do an injustice to the intricacies of both. Nevertheless fulfilment theology, in any of its forms, remains a brave theological attempt to deal with real problems.

(e) Universalisation. Universalisation theology goes one step further than fulfilment theology. Its proponents argue that it is not enough for Christ or the Christian tradition to fulfil others, what is required is that they should include others. Christian theological statements must be universalised in order to genuinely embrace others. The starting point is Christian theology itself and theological premises that are obviously Christian, the goal is that others should be embraced but not smothered by Christian theology. Universalisation theology is the product primarily of Roman Catholic thinkers and it has flourished in the wake of Vatican II.

An early salvo was fired by Hans Küng in a paper given in Bombay in 1964 a week after the *Declaration on Non-Christian Religions* of Vatican II. Entitled *World Religions in God's Plan of Salvation* it made the point that the other religions were part of the history of salvation. Salvation history was universalised to include them. As he put it, 'God is the Lord not only of the special salvation history of the Church but also of that other salvation history: the universal salvation history of all mankind.'[26] Karl Rahner went further than this when he began to use the phrase 'anonymous Christians' of members of other religions. 'Christianity does not simply confront the member of an extra-Christian religion as a mere non-Christian but as someone who can and must already be regarded in this or that respect as an anonymous Christian'.[27] Raimundo Panikkar followed this up by talking about 'the unknown Christ of Hinduism'.

Lying behind universalisation theology there is a cluster of theological ideas. First there is the notion that Christ came to save all humankind. If this is a reasonable theological statement, the question arises as to how in fact does God in Christ save all humankind. For much of humankind lived before the advent of Christ on earth. Moreover in each generation the majority of people are not in a position to hear about Christ. How then can Christ save those who have not been exposed to Him as must be the case if he really did come to save all humanity? The answer is that God provides the means for Christ to save all humankind through the other religious traditions of the world as normal channels of salvation for those within their orbit. Thus it is that Panikkar can talk about the unknown Christ of Hinduism. Second there is the notion that salvation is by faith. The question arises as to what is meant by faith. If by faith is meant not so much correct answers to significant theological questions but authentic quest for transcendence then wherever this is found in all the world religions there is found also, in some measure, salvation by faith. In other words the notion of salvation by faith is universalised from its Christian beginnings to include others. Third there is the notion that there is one God and Mediator, Jesus Christ. At first sight this seems to be an exclusivistic statement that precludes others from the possibility of salvation. The response is that Christ is a universal category. He can no longer be bound by the western Christian limitation introduced by the Greek word Logos, nor can He be bound by the world-view of the human Jesus. He must be universalised to become an authentically universal possibility available outside as well as inside the boundaries of the Christian tradition. In ways such as this, the universalisation theologians universalise orthodox Christian theological categories so that their implications soar beyond the communal armour that seems to enclose them.

Raimundo Panikkar especially has developed an increasing sophistication in his universalisation theology as he has tried to universalise Christ in a meaningful way. Salvation, he claims is centred on Christ but his 'ontic mediatorship . . . is independent of the religion an individual may profess, and from the time and place of his existence on earth, whether inside or outside Christianity, or within or without the historical existence of the visible church'.[28] Christ then saves people but through their own sacraments, and 'as the hidden Messiah or the unknown God, also lives in the hearts of the truly religious men of all religions'.[29] For 'what traditional religious parlance calls the Lord' can be 'what a Hindu may like to call Siva or Visnu, *atman* or *muktidata*, what a Muslim Allah, a Jew Yahweh . . . a Marxist the Future of Humanity, a humanist Truth, a philosopher the Absolute, Absurd, Nothingness, Being and the like'.[30]

Universalisation theology is a heroic intention to preserve Christian theological categories while at the same time taking seriously the religious traditions and faith of others. Christians may grumble that Christian categories are being universalised too far; others may grumble that they do not see an unknown Christ within their own tradition. But, with all its seeming inconsistencies, universalisation theology is an original development within the Christian theological reflection on other religions.

(f) Dialogue. There may be some who would wish to argue that dialogue theology is not so much another theological approach to other religions but a method of contacting other religions. In other words it is not a theological approach in its own right, but a method that can be used with any of the other approaches we have described. There is an element of truth in this. Dialogue is a method, and it may be used with other approaches. At the same time, it has also emerged as an approach that can carry its own theological validity.

Dialogue is a complex notion, both in theory and in practice, and it is necessary first to begin to unravel that complexity. The actual practice of dialogue can happen in a number of ways. First it may happen naturally at grass-roots level. One remembers many occasions in India, on trains or in local situations, where dialogue occurred spontaneously without being organised. Christians such as the White Fathers in North Africa, who subscribe to the notion of 'presence theology', are apt by their very presence in grass-roots situations to become involved in unpremeditated dialogue. This kind of dialogue is also becoming more common in the West as people of other religious traditions become more numerous in western countries. Second dialogue may be induced by governments. This need not sound so outlandish to Christians—after all it was a Roman Emperor, Constantine, who called the bishops to the Council of Nicaea! In places like present-day China, it is the pressure of the local context and the pressure of government that has not only brought Christians together (there are no separate Protestant Churches in China) but has also brought Christians into closer contact with members of other religious traditions. In the third place, inter-religious dialogue may take place at an academic level. This dialogue may be spontaneous and individual, for example at a place such as the Harvard Centre for the Study of World Religions where scholars from different traditions are living and studying together; it may involve academic dialogue between groups of scholars from two separate religious traditions; or it may involve academic dialogue between groups of scholars from many different religious traditions. These different kinds of dialogue—between individuals, between two traditions, between many traditions—are liable to be couched at the academic level of comparative religion, and this, of course, is perfectly natural in the academic milieu. In the fourth place, dialogue may happen between committed Christians and committed members of other religious traditions at the existential or theological level. This can occur outside the sway of religious institutions so that the believers from the different religious traditions are operating freelance in their own capacity rather than as delegates of the Christian Church or Buddhist Sangha, etc. Again this dialogue may be an open-ended meeting between two individuals; it may be a more structured interchange between a group of Christian believers and a group of other believers; or it may be a more structured exchange still between groups drawn from the Christian and various other religious traditions. Dialogue is subtly influenced by size. There is a discernible difference between the dialogue between two individuals, the dialogue between two groups, and the dialogue between many groups. Fifthly and finally, there is the dialogue between representatives of different religious communities. In this kind of setting, the people involved in the dialogue are delegates representing their community and seeking to speak for their community. They are to this extent less free to speak in their own right and in relation to their own personal views. Again this dialogue between representatives may be one between individuals, one between delegates representing two traditions, or one between delegates representing many traditions. The flavour of the dialogue will be different in each case.[31] It is clear therefore that dialogue can take place in many different settings and it will be influenced by them; it can take place between different kinds of people—academics from different traditions, free-lance believers from different traditions, representatives of different traditions—and this will influence the kind of dialogue that takes place; and it can take place between individuals, between groups from two traditions, between groups from many traditions—and this will have an effect upon its nature.

The Christian dialogue with other religions may operate with different theories and goals. At one level the aim may be simply to make contact with and to seek to understand the others. At a recent meeting between the Dalai Lama and Scottish church leaders in Edinburgh, a well known Scottish cleric turned to me and said 'What is the goal of all this?' I replied perhaps the goal is for us to make contact with and to understand the Dalai Lama! The so-called presence theologians, spearheaded by Charles de Foucauld and the White Fathers, and including some of the contributors to the 'Christian Presence' series edited by Max Warren, have spoken to this position.[32] Let us be present with others, is their plea; let us get to know their beliefs; let us see that their religion is deeper than mere propositions; let us listen and try to understand what it means for them to be who they are; let us remember that Christian love propels us to understand them for only so can we love them; let us open up the presence of God in them and so enrich our own sense of God; let us, in some sense, attempt to see the world through their eyes and to understand the universe in the way they understand it. Contact, presence and understanding are therefore the first goal, and they may imply non-verbal dialogue through symbols, art, music, and silence as well as verbal contact.

A second goal of dialogue may be more secular. In the new nations that have emerged since the Second World War, secular concerns such as nation-building have often been important. Christians have joined together with others to take part in secular dialogue with the purpose of sharing with Hindus, Buddhists, Muslims, Jews, etc, the task of nation-building. Dialogue, in this case, was not theological in relation to religious matters, it was secular in regard to economic, political and social matters. The Christian Institute for the Study of Religion and Society at Bangalore in India is one among a number of Christian groups in various lands that has done useful work in secular dialogue as well as in other kinds of dialogue.

A third goal of dialogue may be more conceptual: to establish the facts about other religious traditions in order to avoid overt misunderstandings. There is an overlap here between Religious Studies and Theology for both are seeking to achieve this end from slightly different angles. It is a moot point, that will be discussed later, whether my own work in creating a greater knowledge and understanding of other religions is part of Religious Studies or Theology. It is certainly part of dialogue, and to the benefit of dialogue, if other religions can be better understood conceptually. The old misunderstandings that Hindus worship images rather than the Lord who lies behind them, that Muhammad was an epileptic, that Christians are those who eat beef and drink whisky (as Gandhi once put it)—are removed by this kind of dialogue, and a deeper mutual knowledge is built up. A fourth kind of dialogue is mutual witnessing. At this point there is a division of opinion as to how one should go about this. One Christian viewpoint would argue that before Christians can witness to others they must first understand others. In order to understand it is necessary to put one's own Christian convictions into brackets in order to understand our brother or sister of another tradition. To use technical terms, one should perform *epochē* (putting one's own views into brackets in order to get alongside another) and *Einfühlung* (empathy for the position of another). Having made this effort of understanding, it is only then, the argument goes, that the time is ripe for witnessing to one's own faith. Another Christian viewpoint would suggest that it is psychologically and theologically difficult, if not impossible, to put our convictions into brackets because this would be to imply that our convictions do not matter. The two positions may not be as far apart as they seem.[33] Both would agree that sooner or later the Christian will witness to his or her own position in relation to the position of the partner in dialogue. Dialogue is therefore seen to involve tension as well as agreement, it may open up the real differences between the partners as well as smooth out misunderstandings. At one extreme (less common now than it used to be) this kind of dialogue may have the aim of trying to convert the other. If we understand the partner in dialogue better, so the feeling goes, we will have a better chance of converting him or her. More common is the notion that dialogue involves a mutual learning and even a mutual vulnerability. As Moltmann puts it: 'The dialogue of world religions is a process into which we can only enter if we make ourselves vulnerable in openness, and if we come away from the dialogue changed'.[34] According to this viewpoint, it is not impossible that dialogue may end in conversion, for one partner may be so changed that a switch of religious traditions is the result, but it is more likely that both partners will attain a deeper faith and find deeper riches within their own tradition as the outcome of their dialogue.

At a fifth level, dialogue may involve interchange at an internal spiritual level. It is perhaps no accident that Christian monks such as Bede Griffiths, Thomas Merton, Abhishiktananda (H le Saux), and Aelred Graham have been active in this enterprise. Here dialogue is couched at the level of spirituality. Spiritual preparation for dialogue is stressed on both sides through the reading of the spiritual classics of each tradition, and individual spiritual preparation is made for the dialogue that will ensue. The resulting dialogue will take the form not only of exchange of concepts but also of the mutual understanding and sharing of spiritual riches. This penetrates to a deeper level than academic, theological, or secular dialogue although it may have a spin-off effect upon these other areas.

Finally, though not exhaustively, dialogue can be beneficial for theology. Just as the dialogue with the rediscovered Aristotle enabled Aquinas to deepen his theological understanding and to recast Christian theology in the medieval situation, so too can the dialogue with Hindus, Buddhists, Muslims, Jews, and so on, in different parts of the world enable us to deepen our theological understanding and to recast some of our theological ideas in the modern situation. Indeed the challenge is deeper now. Aristotle when rediscovered remained a western source of renewal. Our present partners in dialogue bring potential treasures from parts of the world that have never yet been tapped by Christian theology but are now available to us in fresh and growing measure. The fruits, as we shall see later, are already being harvested.

Out of the welter of theory and practice that constitutes the Christian dialogue with other religions, an implicit dialogue theology is present. There is the impulse to understand rather than despise or destroy. Understanding arises out of contact and is motivated by Christian love. The understanding sought by different kinds of dialogue theology may take varied forms: understanding theological ideas, understanding spirituality, understanding the faith of others. The meeting with others in order to understand is crucial to the dialogue position. There is also the desire to influence others. Dialogue theology does not rest its case upon passive listening although that will often be present. Witnessing to one's own viewpoint is part of it. Dialogue theology contains the possibility of tension as well as cordiality, of discovering unexpected differences as well as interesting parallels. There is also the willingness to be influenced, and the willingness to grow through dialogue. One's own apprehension of God, one's own awareness of Christ, one's own faith, one's own spirituality, one's traditional theological formulations may be changed or deepened at the same time as hopefully the same thing is happening to one's partner in dialogue. Growth often comes through transpersonal experiences, and dialogue is such an experience *par excellence*. There is also the willingness to learn theologically through dialogue. The Indian experience is a case in point. On the one hand leading Hindus have learnt from Christian theology, men such as Ram Mohan Roy, Keshab Chandra Sen, Vivekananda, Radhakrishnan, Gandhi, and Aurobindo.[35] On the other hand, Christians have benefited by couching Christian theology in Indian thought-forms: de Nobili by using Nyaya philosophy, Appasamy by using Ramanuja's thought, Chenchiah by applying Auro-bindo's ideas, Sadhu Sundar Singh by employing the style of devotional Hinduism. The trickle of theological learning through dialogue is building up into a stream of new insights not only within India but in other parts of the world as well.

For some Christians dialogue may involve undue compromise or invite a diluting of Christian theological truth. It is pre-eminently the approach that encourages contact with others, and in a world that seeks for global understanding that must stand in its favour.

(g) Relativism. We began this survey with exclusivism. We end it at the other end of the theological scale with relativistic theology. According to this, religions are relatively true. They are true relative to the cultures in which they reside, the people who attain faith through them, and the goal toward which they are all advancing. There is no need therefore to think in terms of exclusivism, discontinuity, secularisation, fulfilment, universalisation, or even dialogue. For the latter may involve tension and disagreement. Relativism implies the desire to live and let live. It avoids the necessity of theological ordering of any sort.

The most prominent early modern exponent of this position was Ernst Troeltsch. The relativism of his later years was a theological position, and this distances it from the Religious Studies approach we will look at in the next chapter. Theological relativism is an approach adopted by Christian theologians looking out upon the religious traditions of the rest of the world. In his later work, such as the essay on 'The Place of Christianity Among the World Religions', Troeltsch implies three kinds of theological relativism. The first is cultural relativism. It is the notion that religions are relative to the culture within which they are found. Thus Christianity has been the religious tradition of the western world, Islam has been the religious tradition of the Middle Eastern portion of the world, the Hindu tradition has been the main religious vehicle of India, and the Buddhist tradition has been the dominant religious force in the culture of South East Asia. If one is born into a particular culture it is therefore likely that one will belong to the religious tradition of that culture. Religious traditions are culturally influenced and culturally structured. There is not an 'open sesame' for religious choice and religious belonging whereby one looks into the religious supermarket and makes one's choice from the variety of spiritual goods on display. History and culture must be taken seriously and, as far as Troeltsch was concerned, they point to theological relativism.

The second possibility of theological relativism was epistemological. According to Troeltsch and others who have held this position religious truth is relative to the people who hold it. Christ may be the truth for one person, Krishna may be the truth for another person, Rama may be the truth for another person, the Buddha may be the truth for another person; for other persons truth may be found through the Torah, the Koran, and so on. Religious truth is therefore not absolute for all people everywhere. It is epistemologically relative. Thus Christ, Krishna, Rama, the Buddha, the Torah, the Koran, etc, are not absolutely true for all humankind. They are true as and when persons find them to be true personally. As Troeltsch writes, this need not imply 'any spirit of scepticism or uncertainty. A truth which, in the first instance, is *a truth for us* does not cease, because of this, to be very Truth and Life'.[36] Personal religious truth is therefore saving truth for the person who holds it. Yet although it is authentic truth for that person, it does not follow that it must be so for all humankind.

The third option for theological relativism is teleological. According to this position, religious traditions are different paths. They are not the same. Their ways are separate and do not cross. But their ultimate goal, their *telos*, their end, is the same. Those belonging to different religious traditions are taking journeys along different routes, but their destination is the same. Their tracks may not cross now, but their ultimate direction is towards a common end-point. Religious traditions set out from separate starting-points but they finish in the same place. They are equal paths to the same goal.

Troeltsch's position of 1923 has been refined in recent times by John Hick. His aim is to switch attention from the Christian tradition to the Ultimate Reality that lies beyond all traditions. He states 'that the great world faiths embody different perceptions and conceptions of, and correspondingly different responses to, the Real or the Ultimate from within the major variant cultural ways of being human; and that within each of them the transformation of human existence from self-centeredness to Reality—centeredness is manifestly taking place—and taking place, so far as human observation can tell, to much the same degree.'[37] Hick admits that this implies a different view of Christ. He claims that Christian theology has been moving away from an all-or-nothing notion of Christ to a degree notion of Christ in the thought of Christian theologians such as John Baillie, Donald Baillie, Norman Pittenger, John Knox, Geoffrey Lampe, and in *The Myth of God Incarnate* edited by himself. For him, this opens up the possibility of seeing Christ's mediation of God as being on a par with that accomplished by equivalent mediators in other religious traditions.[38]

Hick suggests that there is the same ineffable Ultimate Reality lying behind all religious traditions. About Ultimate Reality in itself there is little concrete that we can (or should) say. Presumably Ultimate Reality knows what Ultimate Reality is *an sich* (in itself) but this is beyond our human ken. About Ultimate Reality as humanly experienced and thought there is more that can be said. In the different religious traditions the experience of Ultimate Reality can be seen in two ways. It can be seen on the one hand as the Real, or God, as personal; it can be seen on the other hand as the Real, or Absolute, as non-personal. The Real, or God, as personal can be seen in the Christian Father God, the Jewish Yahweh, the Muslim Allah, the Hindu Krishna, and so on; the Real, or Absolute, as non-personal can be seen in the

Hindu Brahman, the Buddhist Nirvana, the Taoist Tao, and so on. These expressions of the Real are independently valid. Thus, as far as Hick is concerned, the Christian theological approach to other religious traditions will not be one of competition but the 'mutual mission of the sharing of insights and experiences'.[39] This is full-blooded religious pluralism and theological relativism.

Clearly this viewpoint gives full weight and integrity to the other religious traditions. The question is does it do full justice to Christian theology? It has close similarities to some aspects of Hindu thought, although even then Advaita Vedanta would claim that its own view of the Real, or Absolute, as non-personal is *higher* than the view that the Real, or God, is personal. The theological relativistic, view of Christ is problematical and would not be accepted by the majority of Christians. It has the appearance of being a somewhat abstract exercise in the theology of religion rather than a summing-up of where the Christian community around the world actually *is* in regard to this matter. After all, with the spread of *all* the religious traditions of the world into other cultures in the movement of peoples around the world since World War Two, all religions are more universal and less culture-bound than they once were. Cultural relativism does not have the force that it once had. Local Christians engaged in mission in local situations in India, Africa, Japan, Latin America, and so on are the cutting-edge of the Christian tradition in the modern world. Their voice must increasingly be heard and it is by no means clear that their voice favours theological relativism.

3. CONCLUSION

We have briefly outlined seven Christian theological attitudes to other religious traditions. It would have been possible to include many more examples within each section had there been more space. For example William Ernest Hocking's notion of reconception is important and it hovers between fulfilment of essence, and universalisation and dialogue theology.[40] What we have said in passing about Hocking is also more widely true. Few authors fall utterly and completely within the sole orbit of one theological attitude. It is especially the case that dialogue theology can often be combined with another approach.

Nevertheless one may dare to say that all the possible theological attitudes to other religious traditions fall somewhere within the spectrum of views that we have outlined above.

The work of our last-mentioned author, John Hick, takes us over into the work of Wilfred Cantwell Smith who influenced Hick. It raises the question of whether religious pluralism and a theology of religion properly belong within the orbit of Christian theology, or whether they belong somewhere else. It raises the question of the relationship between Christian theology and Religious Studies.

FOOTNOTES

1. W C Smith, *The Meaning and End of Religion*, New American Library, New York, 1966.
2. Edward W Said, *Orientalism*, Routledge & Kegan Paul, London, 1978.
3. See Hans Küng's formulation of the problem in 'The World Religions in God's Plan of Salvation', pp 31–37, in J Neuner, (ed.), *Christian Revelation and World Religions*, Burns and Oates, London, 1967.
4. See B B Warfield, *The Inspiration and Authority of the Bible*, Marshall, Morgan and Scott, London, 1951.
5. K Barth, *Church Dogmatics*, ed. G W Bromiley and T F Torrance, T & T Clark, Edinburgh, 1956, Vol 1 Part 2, p 303.
6. H Kraemer, *The Christian Message in a Non-Christian World*, Edinburgh House Press, London, 1938, p 135.
7. H Kraemer, *Religion and the Christian Faith*, Lutterworth, London, 1956, p 83.
8. *Ibid*, p 82.
9. H Kraemer, *The Christian Message in a Non-Christian World*, Edinburgh House Press, London, 1938, p 135.
10. E Brunner, *Revelation and Reason*, SCM Press, London, 1947, p 270.
11. A Th. van Leeuwen, *Christianity and World History*, Charles Scribner's Sons, New York, 1964, p 331.
12. *Ibid*, p 332.
13. *Ibid*, pp 419–420.
14. E Laszlo, *The Inner Limits of Mankind*, Pergamon, Oxford, 1978, p 3.
15. H Cox, *Turning East*, Simon and Schuster, New York, 1977.

16. See O C Thomas, *Attitudes Toward Other Religions*, Harper & Row, New York, 1969, pp 21–22.

17. J N Farquhar, *The Crown of Hinduism*, Humphrey Milford, London, 1913, p 33.

18. R C Zaehner, *The Comparison of Religions*, Beacon Paperback, Boston, 1962, p 180.

19. R C Zaehner, *Concordant Discord*, Clarendon, Oxford, 1970, p 363.

20. *Ibid*, p 363.

21. *Ibid*, p 363.

22. *Ibid*, p 359.

23. *Ibid*, p 355.

24. *Ibid*, p 360.

25. See F Whaling, 'Srī Aurobindo: A Critique' in *The Journal of Religious Studies*, vol VII, 1979, No. 2, pp 66–103.

26. H Kung, 'The World Religions in God's Plan of Salvation', in J Neuner, (ed.), *Christian Revelation and World Religions*, Burns & Oates, London, 1967, p 52.

27. K Rahner, *Theological Investigations*, Vol V, Darton Longman & Todd, London, 1966, p 131.

28. R Panikkar, 'The Relation of Christians to their non-Christian Surroundings' in J Neuner, (ed.), *Christian Revelation and World Religions*, Burns & Oates, London, 1967, p 164.

29. R Panikkar, in *Religion and Society*, XV, September 1968, p 49.

30. R Panikkar, 'Christianity and World Religions', in *Christianity*, Punjabi University, Patiala, 1969, p 100.

31. Useful background works are:– C F Hallencreutz, *Dialogue and Community*, Swedish Institute of Missionary Research, Uppsala, 1977; Eric J Sharpe, *Faith Meets Faith*, SCM Press, London, 1977; F Whaling, *An Approach to Dialogue: Christianity and Hinduism*, Lucknow Publishing House, Lucknow, 1966.

32. See especially:– K. Cragg, *Sandals at the Mosque*, SCM Press, London, 1959; R Hammer, *Japan's Religious Ferment*, SCM Press, London, 1961; J V Taylor, *The Primal Vision*, SCM Press, London, 1963; W Stewart, India's Religious Frontier, SCM Press, London, 1964.

33. See for example Abhishiktananda, 'The Way of Dialogue' in H Jai Singh, (ed.), *Inter-Religious Dialogue*, CISRS, Bangalore, 1967, pp 86–90; S Neill, *Crises of Belief*, Hodder & Stoughton, London, 1984.

34. Quoted in John Hick & Brian Hebblethwaite, (eds.), *Christianity and other Religions*, Collins, London, 1980, p 194.

35. See M M Thomas, *The Acknowledged Christ of the Indian Renaissance*, SCM Press, London, 1969.

36. E Troeltsch, *Christian Thought: its History and Application*, University of London Press, London, 1923, p 34.

37. John Hick, 'Religious Pluralism' in F Whaling, (ed.), *The World's Religious Traditions: Current Perspectives in Religious Studies*, T & T Clark, Edinburgh, 1984, p 156.

38. *Ibid*, pp 154–5.

39. *Ibid*, p 164.

40. See W E Hocking, *Living Religions and a World Faith*, Macmillan, New York, 1940.

CHAPTER FIVE

TWO GLOBAL VIEWS OF WORLD RELIGIONS: CHRISTIAN THEOLOGY OR RELIGIOUS STUDIES?

I. INTRODUCTION

In this chapter we switch our attention to the global attitude to world religions indicated in the title of this book. We will look at two of the most interesting and important attempts since World War Two to take a global perspective towards world religions. They centre on the work of Wilfred Cantwell Smith who is now recognised as one of the key figures in this area, and the equally important insights of the *philosophia perennis* (perennial philosophy) school. Both schools of thought have begun to come into their own in recent years.

They both share an interest in theology and world religions. Indeed both are berated from opposite directions. Some Christian theologians accuse Smith of being too historical and comparative, and *philosophia perennis* of being too mystical; some Religious Studies scholars accuse Smith of being too concerned with theology, and *philosophia perennis* of being too concerned with philosophy; other Religious Studies experts accuse both Smith and *philosophia perennis* of being too interested in transcendence. Hidden behind these comments are implicit views of what Christian theology, theology, and Religious Studies basically are.

The work of Wilfred Cantwell Smith and the *philosophia perennis* school raise basic questions namely What is Christian Theology? and What is Religious Studies? Is the work of these two approaches part of Christian Theology, part of Religious Studies, or part of both? What do we mean by Christian Theology and World Religions?

2. WILFRED CANTWELL SMITH

(a) Background. Smith's serious academic work began when he was at Lahore in Muslim India from 1941–1949. It was then that he began his ongoing study of Islam and his ongoing contact with Muslims. This engagement with Islam was continued when he founded and led the McGill Institute of Islamic Studies in 1951. This Institute brought together equal numbers of western and Muslim students and faculty. It was clear from the start that here was someone who, although a Christian and in time an ordained Christian minister, was willing to study Islam seriously and to take Muslims seriously as persons.

In 1959 Smith wrote an important article, *Comparative Religion: Whither and Why?* In it he made reference to eight important points that were to influence the rest of his work: stress upon persons rather than things, his concern to understand other religious traditions, an awareness that religious truth has to do with inward faith as well as outward tradition, an intuition that the study of religion is a global affair that has to do with the whole of humanity, a perception that transcendence is a crucial part of the subject matter of religion, an emphasis upon dialogue and especially what he called colloquium between religious traditions, a conviction that the study of religion belongs to the greater whole of humane knowledge, and an insistence that the views of members of other religious traditions are a substantial contribution to that greater whole. These themes were drawn out in his later work notably at Harvard (1964–1973 and 1978–1984). Let us then look in more detail at what Smith has to say about Christian Theology and World Religions.

(b) God and Humanity. In fact the twin presuppositions of Smith's work, his two dominant themes, are not Christian Theology and World Religions but God and humanity. For Smith, both God and humanity are 'given' while other things, including religious traditions, are in flux. God and humankind are the starting-point and the foundation of thought. Everything else fits into the framework given by the constants of God and humanity. To put it in another way, Smith's initial intuition is global. God and humanity are global universals.

While other things may change, transcendence and human nature are abiding realities. It is easy to see how Hick has moulded his thought upon that of Smith. For Smith does not start with Christian theology, the Christian tradition, or any other tradition, he starts with God and humanity and works from them and the global world they imply back to the religious traditions. Thus, 'religious life begins in the fact of God: a fact that includes His initiative, His agony, His love for all of us without exception . . . Given that fact—and it is given; absolutely, and quite independently of whether or how we human beings recognise it; given that irremovable fact, religious life then consists in the quality of our response'.[3] God is then the given, the constant, the presupposition of religious life and study; and what responds to God is not any of the religious traditions directly (after all Christianity or Hinduism never saved anybody) but human persons.

There are similarities between Smith's thought and that of Martin Buber who also stressed an I–Thou personalism between God and persons, and human beings in their own relationships. Persons are very important in Smith's thought. Religious traditions consist of persons, and are formed and changed by persons. Humanity itself in the form of persons has priority over the collectivities, including religious traditions, that are formed by humanity to express its common life[4].

(c) *Religion and religions*. Where then do religious traditions fit into Smith's thought? If they are not primary, what is their importance? In The *Meaning and End of Religion*, Smith threw a bombshell into the academic world by asserting that the two terms 'religion' and 'religions' are obsolete. 'Neither religion in general nor any one of the religions', Smith contended, 'is in itself an intelligible entity, a valid object of enquiry or concern either for the scholar or for the man of faith'[5]. There is a curious parallel, at this point, between Smith and Barth. Both want to do away with 'religion'. However their reasons for doing away with religion are opposed. Barth felt that religion was tantamount to unbelief, it was humanity's attempt to try and capture and bring down God. Whereas the initiative lay with God and His revelation which was discontinuous with human religion, which amounted to human efforts to search out God. Smith too wanted to emphasise God and his revelation at the expense of religion. But for him revelation is not limited to the Word made manifest in Christ, it is open to all people through the medium of their own religious traditions. All men and women have an innate capacity for faith, and for him this is not 'religion' it is part of the human birthright. His problem with 'religion' is that it tends to set up blocks between God and humanity's response to God. Religion becomes an entity in itself rather than a means to an end; religion is seen as having an essence and therefore becomes an absolute instead of a community on the move; the emphasis comes to be placed upon religions rather than the communication between human beings and God, as though religions have any saving grace, power, or meaning apart from the persons who constitute them. In a penetrating analysis of the word 'religion' from Roman times until now, Smith concludes that it has been used in four different ways: as personal piety, or religiousness; as a generic term, or religion in general; as an outward particular religion seen as an ideal, as in 'true Christianity'; and as an outward particular religion seen in practice, as in the 'Christianity of history'. Smith suggests that 'the word, and the concepts, should be dropped—at least in all but the first, personalist, sense', and that 'the term 'religion' is confusing, unnecessary, and distorting'.[6] In making this audacious statement, Smith is not opposing religion to revelation, or implying that the other religions are humanity's unavailing attempts to capture God. Far from it! He is implying that true 'religion' in the sense of personal piety *IS* the human response to God in all the religious traditions of the world. The trouble is that scholars and people of faith have, for reasons located in the western intellectual world since the Enlightenment, reified religion and made it into a thing separate from humanity and God so that, in its state of suspended animation, it has become a confused and distorted obstacle to the operation of true 'religion'. Smith is therefore questioning the use of the word 'religion' and the words for the 'religions' (Hinduism, Buddhism, Christianity etc), not in order to condemn human faith in transcendence, but in order to save it.

(d) Faith and tradition. To replace the terms 'religion' and 'religions', Smith introduces his own terms 'faith' and 'tradition'. By faith, he writes, 'I mean personal faith . . . an inner religious experience or involvement of a particular person; the impingement upon him of the transcendent, puta-tive or real'.[7] By tradition, he writes, 'I mean the entire mass of overt objective data that constitute the historical deposit, as it were, of the past religious life of the community in question: temples, scriptures, theological systems, dance patterns, legal and other social institutions, conventions, moral codes, myths, and so on; anything that can be and is transmitted from one person, one generation, to another, and that an historian can observe'.[8] For Smith these are all-embracing terms. 'It is my suggestion, he writes, 'that by the use of these two notions it is possible to conceptualise and to describe anything that has ever happened in the religious life of mankind'.[9]

(e) Implications for Christian Theology and World Religions. What then are the implications of Smith's work for Christian theology and world religions in the global situation? The consequences of his work are subtle and our space is limited, so we will try to be both brief and relevant.

In the first place, theology is not plural but one. Theology is a global exercise. It does not, as it were, start from within the boundaries of particular religious traditions and look out upon the world with the spectacles of Christian, Jewish, Muslim, Hindu, Buddhist, or any other particular theologies. The parameters of theology are global and they include the theologies of particular religious traditions within a wider whole. Theology, in other words, looks back from its global perspective in the direction of particular theologies as opposed to beginning with the theological assumptions of particular religious traditions and proceeding from them in the direction of a more universalistic theology. Smith's position, in short, is not that of the universalisation theology we looked at in the last chapter which begins with the premises of one tradition and universalises those premises to include others.

He assumes that theology is global and one, because God and humanity are global and one, and he incorporates particular theological insights into a theology that is universal at the start and in principle. There is no need to try to make theology global and universal—it is so anyway. According to this viewpoint, the theology of religions must be the product of someone who sees, and feels, and indeed knows, persons of all religious traditions to be ultimately members of one community, one in which they all participate. Because this is so, Smith has been keen to search for universal theological categories that are common to all the religious traditions of the world and are not merely the product of one. He has experimented so far with the notions of faith, tradition, participation, and religious truth as being universal theological categories that are applicable to all the religious traditions. In short the theology of religions includes at the same time as it transcends particular theologies; a theology of religions must be Christian; but it must not be a Christian theology. In other words, according to Smith, a theology of religions should not be that of a particular religious community looking out upon the others and saying how can we understand, reject, or incorporate you; a theology of religions should be Christian, Hindu, Muslim, Jewish, Buddhist, etc, as such.[10]

This leads us on to our second point. Smith's contention is that nouns divide, and adjectives unite. Thus when Christianity, Islam, Judaism, Hinduism, Buddhism, etc, operate as nouns they imply separation and division between the traditions that are named. However when adjectives are used, such as Christian, Muslim, Jewish, Hindu, Buddhist, etc, there is no longer division and separation. Indeed it is possible to talk about a Muslim Christian in the sense of a Christian who is submitted (as the word Muslim implies) to God, and so on. It is possible also to talk (as we saw above) about a theology of religions that is Christian, Buddhist, etc, but when the small word 'a' is added and we pass on to discourse about a Christian theology, a Jewish theology, a Muslim theology, a Hindu theology, etc, adjectives are, so to speak, turned into nouns which are separate rather than joined. It seems to me, at this point, that Smith is becoming ambivalent. In his concern to stress the global nature of theology and to counteract any theological particularity that may introduce a jarring note he is weakening his argument. What does it mean to use the words Christian, Muslim, Jewish, Hindu and Buddhist in his adjectival sense? Insofar as particularism is excluded, it can only mean that they are left with a vague, indistinct, ethical meaning. It would be better to keep the natural meanings, i.e. that Christian theology is the theology that is held by the Christian tradition, Muslim theology is the theology that is held by the Muslim tradition, and so on. This meaning need not contradict his theological globalism. The point is that, in any way possible, Smith is anxious to make the point that 'in principle there is but one truth about the whole religious life of mankind, whether it has been lived in Buddhist or Christian forms'.[11]

This raises a third point namely that while Smith's concept is admirable is it in fact Christian theology? This depends, of course, upon what we mean by Christian theology. We return to our discussion on the meaning of the word theology in chapter three. We saw that there are basically three possibilities: theology is not anchored in a religious tradition but is part of a general education which must include some 'knowledge of God' as well as knowledge of other matters (Greece and Rome); theology is anchored in and produced by a religious tradition (medieval Christendom); and theology is not anchored in one religions tradition but it bestraddles them all in a theology of religions (Smith). Smith is a prophet who is trying to nudge us beyond the second view of theology in the direction of the third. His promptings invite three responses. The first is the somewhat naive sociological point that most persons of faith begin their reflection on these matters not from a global perspective but from within the roots of their own community. Smith's prophetic soundings may be fulfilled in the future, but at this juncture in history most religious people work from within their tradition towards a global position rather than the other way round. For them Christian theology is the theology of the Christian tradition rather than a sub-species of global theology. Roots are important. Smith is one of the great personalists of our time together with the likes of Martin Buber and Paul Tournier

but in his desire to upgrade personal faith he may be inclined
to downgrade the power of traditions to structure personal
faith. Secondly, his presuppositions that God and humanity
are primary, given, and constant are just that—philosophical
presuppositions. They are not self-evident. Indeed it is possible, as in my own model, to point out that there is a transcendent Reality lying beyond all religious traditions, there is a
mediating focus present in all religious traditions, and there is
a faith orientation underlying all religious traditions without
presupposing that they have the same form, weight and value.
That may prove to be the case but it needs to be developed
academically, not taken for granted. Thirdly and perhaps
most importantly it would appear to be the case that there
are two different academic enterprises engaged in discussing
this matter, on the one hand Christian theology, and on the
other hand Religious Studies. Smith's direct concern is not
with Christian theology *per se* but with Religious Studies. His
concern is not with dialogue as such but with colloquium.
There is a difference between engaging in dialogue and in
chairing a dialogue between others. There is a difference
between conceptualising the thought of a religious tradition
in movement and in observing all traditions, including one's
own, in a critical, disciplined, intellectually rigorous,
empirical and academic way. This is roughly the difference
between Christian theology (when theology is applied to the
Christian tradition) and Religious Studies. Smith's basic
sympathies are with the latter.

This raises a more radical point, our fourth in all, as to
whether Smith's work is properly termed theological. When
we talk about his theology of religions, is theology the right
term to use? We saw in chapter three that theology retains
as its primary meaning knowledge of or talk about God. To
what extent is Smith concerned with this? In fact he says very
little about God. God may be given, but little content is given
to God. 'Faith', he writes, is concerned with something, or
Someone, behind or beyond Christianity, or Buddhism'.[12] But
that something, or Someone is left vague. Indeed deliberately
so far God is ineffable, 'God is a reality about which none of
us knows enough to be dogmatic or scurrilous; yet about
which each of us may, through his own symbols and his own

faith, know enough to live—and indeed live in a way that is transcendently final'.[13] For Smith there is little future in attempting to define or conceptualise God who is not observable. There is more mileage in investigating what can be seen, namely the religious traditions of humankind and the faith that creates and sustains them. God remains as an *a priori* assumption, but by far the greatest amount of time is spent on the personal life of humanity; other discussions derive from that. But if there is little talk about God and much talk about humankind's faith and religiousness, are we left with theology? Smith's so-called universal theological categories faith, tradition, participation and religious truth are to do with humanity, not with God. Are they then theological categories?

The waters have been muddied by a group of scholars within Religious Studies who felt that the study of religion should concentrate upon empirical, historical, sociological, phenomenological, anthropological, psychological, and philological studies. Their concern was that the discipline should be seen to be scientifically respectable in the academic world. They therefore eschewed mention of transcendental dimensions, of theology, and often of philosophy because they were convinced that these areas of discussion were beyond the true bounds of Religious Studies. In their eyes, any talk of God, any reference to dialogue, automatically labelled Smith as a theologian even though he rarely mentioned God, and was interested in colloquium rather than dialogue.[14]

(f) Conclusions. It is clear that Smith and scholars like him are on the hinterland between Christian theology and Religious Studies, and the time has come for us to draw some tentative conclusions as a result of the discussion in this chapter. Our first conclusion is that Christian theology remains primarily the theology arising out of the Christian tradition. Smith's attempt to convert theology into a global discipline that is universal (on the lines of other academic disciplines that are in principle universal) belongs essentially to another academic enterprise that we may term Religious Studies. The words 'Christian Theology' therefore refer to the theology of Christians and do, to that extent, have a particular connotation.

Together with the theologies of other religious traditions Christian theology may contribute to a coming world theology of religions. But this must be worked for, and it cannot be assumed (at any rate at the theological level) that it is globally given.

Our second conclusion is that Religious Studies is wider than Christian theology (or theology in general). It includes the study of all the religious traditions of the world and it includes methodological approaches from within the Social Sciences and Humanities such as history, sociology, anthropology, linguistics, psychology, phenomenology, and the study of myths and texts. However Religious Studies need not be confined to the humane and social sciences. It is essentially the study of humanity in its religious dimension. Discussion of transcendence and personal faith are therefore by no means irrelevant to Religious Studies. Transcendence and personal faith are on the agenda of the *non*-theological study of religion.

Our third conclusion is that we are faced with a problem of terminology in this discussion. This is complicated by Smith's use of the terms 'God' and 'theology'. What he calls God refers to not only the Christian view of God, but also to the Muslim view of Allah, the Jewish view of Yahweh, the Hindu view of Brahman, and the Buddhist view of Nirvana. God is therefore a kind of analogue for transcendence. What Smith calls universal theological categories could equally be called universal philosophical categories, or universal comparative religious categories. They are to do with the global religiousness of humanity, and the fact that transcendence is seen to lie behind them does not, of itself, convert them into *theological* categories. What we have here is not therefore so much a theology of religions as a *theoria*, a universal theory, of world religions.

It is an attractive theory that takes the world's religious traditions seriously and gives due weight to transcendence and personal faith. It finds its authentic place within an integral Religious Studies rather than within Christian theology. As such it can influence Christian theology but it does so from within a different area of concern. In other words the perspective upon world religions taken by Christian theology and Religious Studies is different. The two areas may overlap but they are not to be confused.

3. PHILOSOPHIA PERENNIS

(a) Background. During this century, and especially since World War Two, a loosely-allied group of scholars has come into being which owes a general allegiance to the school of thought known as *philosophia perennis*, or the perennial philosophy. This viewpoint, like Smith's, takes the world's religious traditions seriously, has a global outlook, and holds a clear notion of transcendence. In important details it differs from Smith, but like him it overlaps Christian theology and world religions. We will look at it now mainly through the eyes of two of its foremost present-day exponents, Huston Smith and Seyyed Hossein Nasr.[15]

Mention of Nasr's name indicates that this school diverges from any we have looked at before in that two of its finest representatives, Nasr and Ananda Coomaraswamy, are respectively a Muslim and a Hindu.[16] However most of the school are westerners or Christians, and they have all grappled with the basic question of Christian theology and world religions.

(b) What is the perennial philosophy? This is a hazardous question to raise in the context of a short chapter, and I can imagine my colleagues Seyyed Hossein Nasr and Huston Smith groaning inwardly as they prepare to read a swift summary of what their work is all about! To quote Aldous Huxley, it is

> the metaphysic that recognises a divine Reality substantial to the world of things and lives and minds; the psychology that finds in the soul something similar to, or even identical with, divine Reality; the ethic that places man's final end in the knowledge of the immanent and transcendent Ground of all being.[17]

This statement from Huxley's early and popular work illustrates the importance of transcendence for *philosophia perennis*.

Transcendent Reality itself matters deeply, as do the echoes of transcendence that are found in the human soul. To this extent, *philosophia perennis* is on a similar wavelength to that of Wilfred Cantwell Smith for whom the concepts of God and humanity were the key to the religious life of humankind. This school also starts with a global view of Ultimate Reality and of human nature and works from this starting-point to the religious traditions of the world. Like Smith, it works from the global to the particular; it works from a universal view of the divine being and human beings to actual religious communities. Yet at the same time, like Smith, it gives a high if relative importance to religious traditions. Religions matter because it is in practice through them that the perennial philosophy becomes available to persons. Moreover, insofar as they are not pseudo-religions, 'there is not the question of which religion is "better" since all authentic religions come from the same origin'.[18] In other words, Christianity has no head-start over other traditions. It has the same access as others to the *philosophia perennis*. It has the same grounding in Absolute Reality as other religious traditions. As Nasr puts it:

> The conception of religion in the school of the *philosophia perennis* is vast enough to embrace the primal and the historical, the Semitic and the Indian, the mythic and the 'abstract' types of religions ... making it possible to develop a veritable theology of comparative religion—which in reality should be called metaphysics of comparative religion—able to do theological justice to the tenets of each religion while enabling the student of religion, who is at once interested objectively in the existence of religions other than his own and is at the same time of a religious nature himself, to cross frontiers as difficult to traverse as that which separates the world of Abraham from that of Kṛṣṇa and Rāma or the universe of the American Indians from that of traditional Christianity.[19]

Clearly therefore in some important respects *philosophia perennis* converges with Wilfred Cantwell Smith's approach. The perennial philosophy that lies at the heart of all traditions is analogous to Smith's view of faith; the Absolute Reality of *philosophia perennis* corresponds to Smith's view of God; in both cases Absolute Reality, God, is 'given'; in both positions, transcendence is crucial; a theology of religion is present within both viewpoints; both raise the cry 'let religion be religion' to save it from being reduced to anything else; and both emphasise the role played by religious traditions as the channels that enable humans to appropriate the Divine.

(c) Hierarchy. However *philosophia perennis* adopts a position that is different from as well as similar to that of Smith. In the first place, the exponents of the perennial philosophy place a greater stress upon hierarchy. For them, there are different levels and layers of reality and being, and nothing is gained by confusing them. These levels are fourfold. At the highest level, there is the unmanifest God at the infinite level of reality; secondly there is the manifest God at the celestial level of reality; thirdly there is the world in its invisible aspect of mind; and finally there is the world in its visible aspect of material existence. The interesting thing about this analysis is that the fourth level, which is stressed and studied most in our modern world, is seen to be the least important. It stands at the bottom of the hierarchy and is given meaning by the levels that lie above. It is best studied through the medium of the natural sciences with their emphasis upon number, controlled experiment, prediction, and objectivity. However, what this visible material world and the natural sciences that study it cannot reveal are values, purposes, life meanings, and quality. They belong to a higher level.

These four levels of reality correspond to four different levels within the human self. At the lowest level comes body, followed by mind, soul, and spirit. In commenting upon this, Huston Smith writes:

A life that identifies primarily with its physical pleasures and needs ('getting and spending we lay waste our days') is superficial; one that advances its attention to mind can be interesting; if it moves on to the heart (synonym for soul) it can be good; and if it passes on to spirit—that saving self-forgetfulness and egalitarianism in which one's personal interests loom no larger than those of others—it would be perfect.[20]

We will not comment upon this hierarchical scheme at the moment. The important thing is to realise that it lies at the heart of *philosophia perennis* and that at the higher levels spirit comes higher than soul, realisation of the unmanifest God higher than realisation of the manifest God.

(d) Spirituality. Secondly there lies implicit in the viewpoint of this school an awareness of the importance of spirituality, especially mystical spirituality. The fourth level of spirit is essentially the level of the unmanifest God, it is the level of mysticism. At this point one passes beyond a relationship with a personal God. Concerning this highest level Huston Smith states, 'looking up from planes that are lower, God is radically transcendent (*ganz Anders*; wholly other); looking down, from heights that human vision (too) can to varying degrees attain, God is absolutely immanent'.[21] In spite of this stress upon mysticism it is true to say that *philosophia perennis* emphasises, in their due place, all the facets of religion. It gives an honoured place to all the elements in my model: religious community, ritual, ethics, social involvement, scripture/myth, concepts, aesthetics, and spirituality. However, among these, spirituality is more equal than the others because it provides better access to deeper levels of the Godhead and of the human self.

(e) Transcendent unity of religions. Thirdly the school of *philosophia perennis* thinks in terms of the transcendent unity of all religions. At the level of the unmanifest God, at the level of the eternal part of the self, there is an ultimate unity. At this level the differences between religious traditions pale into insignifance. Within the perspective of transcendent Reality, differences of religious community, ritual, ethics, social involvement, scripture, concepts, and aesthetics—although only too apparent—are seen to be unimportant. However, and it is important to grasp this in order to understand the perennial philosophy, at the outward level religious traditions are varied and unique. It is the glory of religious traditions that they have their own stamp, their own sociological and

historical outworkings, their own psychological imprint. Absolute Reality may be absolute, the transcendent Origin of religions may be one, the Primordial Tradition may be unitary, the *philosophia perennis* may be inwardly the same; by the same token 'the logos, prophet, sacred book, avatar or some other direct manifestation of the Divinity in different religions[22] is *relatively* absolute, the descents from the Origin are different, the religious traditions that derive from the Primordial Tradition are unique, the outward expressions of the pure light of *philosophia perennis* reflect the varied beauty of all the colours of the rainbow. Thus although inwardly there is a transcendent unity of all the religions, outwardly they are very different. And this is seen to be a virtue and a glory. There is no need for religious traditions to abandon their own beliefs, their own orthodoxy, their own uniqueness in order to accomodate to others in our global world. At the outward level diversity reigns, at the inward level unity is the order of the day. It is in the light of this framework that Nasr is able to chide John Hick for, as it would seem to Nasr, weakening his Christology in order accomodate the religious pluralism of our global age.

Clearly the above summary of the viewpoint of *philosophia perennis* has been all too rapid, as was the case with our description of the work of Wilfred Cantwell Smith. More space and nuancing would be required to do full justice to these two important approaches to the relationship between Christian theology and world religions. I hope it is evident from what has been said that they are interesting and significant contributions to this debate. What then can we say about the *philosophia perennis* position within the context of this book?

Let it be said first that this school provides a neat solution to the question that lies before us. It takes Christian orthodoxy seriously, and at the same time it gives due weight to the authentic nature of all the world's religious traditions. In so doing it devotes attention to the nature of divine reality and so spends a lot of time upon the foremost task of theology as classically conceived. Its scholars have done splendid work both upon particular religious traditions in their breadth and depth and upon the inter-relations between different religious traditions. There is some substance therefore in their claim that their work is not taken with the seriousness it deserves. It may well be the case that some of the people reading this book have never heard of the *philosophia perennis* school, and I hope that this introduction will lead to more dialogue and interaction between colleagues in the *philosophia perennis* school and other colleagues in theology and Religious Studies.

(f) Implications.

(i) Importance of spirituality. In closing this chapter let me make four comments upon the *philosophia perennis* viewpoint from my own perspective in order to bring out their contribution to the debate that lies at the heart of this book. In the first place, they emphasise the importance of spirituality. In so doing they resonate with a growing feeling in varied religious and intellectual circles that the discussion of our global problems is couched at a too outward and intellectual level. Recent courses in spirituality at universities around the world are attracting larger-than-expected numbers of students. Recent publishing initiatives in the area of spirituality, for example *The classics of western spirituality*[23] published by the Paulist Press and *World spirituality: an encyclopaedic history of the religious quest*[24] projected by the Crossroad Press, are finding a ready response. However it is one thing to place more emphasis upon spirituality—the question is whether too much emphasis is being placed upon spirituality. Christian theology in general, it may be admitted, has often undervalued spirituality so that the other elements in my model of what constitutes a religious tradition (religious community, ritual, ethics, social involvement, scripture/myth, concepts, and aesthetics) have tended to receive more weight than spirituality. It is good that the balance should be put right and in this book due stress is placed upon concepts and spirituality as being central within the concerns of Christian theology. The tendency within *philosophia perennis* is to place disproportionate stress upon spirituality so that it is seen to be not merely one among eight elements which together constitute a religious tradition but rather *the* element that matters most to the extent that it is placed at a higher level than the other

elements. At this stage it becomes not one among a cluster of more-or-less equal elements but the normative element in the light of which all the other elements receive their significance. It may be asked at this point whether the praiseworthy attempt to bring out the authentic importance of spirituality has not been taken too far.

(ii) Transcendence and global thinking. In the second place, the school of perennial philosophy stresses transcendence both within humanity and within the Godhead. And this emphasis is important for thinking globally. It is interesting to trace the evolution of global thinking in the last fifteen years and to see how the perspectives of global thought converge with *philosophia perennis.* The trigger to much recent thinking about our global situation was provided by the original Club of Rome report which highlighted in a spectacular way the emerging problems of humanity in regard to areas such as energy, world population, natural resources, food production, ecology, pollution, climate, and urbanisation. The first reaction to this report was to assume that the global problems produced by science and technology could be solved by science and technology. The feeling was that a greater finesse and financing of technological research could rectify the dilemmas that same research had produced, and that our global problems were mainly ecological and physical and could therefore be solved by better technology.[25] By the end of the 1970's, the partial nature of this thinking had become clear to many. It came to be seen that the root causes even of physical and ecological problems lay elsewhere, for example in the inner constraints on our vision and values. In other words, lying behind science and technology were the human values that gave rise to science and technology, and what was needed was a new view of humanity and a new vision of a set of humane values and insights that could produce personal and cultural vistas that would take us beyond the limitations produced by science and technology. The clue lay not so much in nature and the natural sciences but in humanity and the human sciences![26] Recently—and here we come to the distinctive contribution made to this debate

by *philosophia perennis*—a third strand has been added to the discussion, namely that of transcendence. The original strand had emphasised nature and body; the second strand had stressed humanity and mind; the third strand highlighted the transcendent elements of Absolute Reality and soul and spirit. Lying behind body and mind were soul and spirit. Lying behind nature and humanity were the manifest and unmanifest God. Body and mind found their real significance in the light of soul and spirit. Nature and humanity became ultimately meaningful in the light of transcendence. Such were the intuitions of *philosophia perennis* as filtered through the Global Premises Project of Willis Harman and similar lenses.[27] They added a third transcendental dimension to the global debate. In so doing, they indirectly highlighted the absence of a strong stress on transcendence in Christian theology, the virtual absence of Christian theology from the global debate, and the need for Christian theology to reorientate some of its concerns in order to become truly involved in global thinking. An obvious instance of this is the imperative upon Christian theology to grapple with and renew itself through the other world religions, the dialogue with which throws it 'willynilly' into the business of involvement in wider global considerations.

(iii) Wider context of Christian theology and world religions. In the third place, the school of perennial philosophy raises the question of the inter-relationship between Christian theology and Religious Studies within a wider context. During western intellectual history three educational models have been thrown up during different periods that correspond to the three strands we have just examined, namely nature, humanity, and transcendence—or body, mind, and soul/spirit. As we saw in chapter three, the Greeks and Romans stressed what they called *humanitas*, what we call the Humanities. Their focus was upon humanity. Their genius was for humane studies. Their concern was for the subjects that were relevant to humankind. Their concentration was therefore upon literature, other languages, history, geography, philosophy, maths and

rhetoric, and their assumption was that true learning contributed to the moral, political and general welfare of humanity. Within *humanitas*, the natural sciences and theology had their own role. But it was a supporting role rather than a dominant one. The key lay in humankind and the Humanities rather than in nature and the natural sciences or in transcendence and theology. The welfare of human beings (provided they weren't slaves) was what mattered and, as Aristotle put it, a person with *humanitas* was one who in his own person was able to judge critically in all or nearly all branches of knowlege and not merely in some special subject.

During the period of medieval Christendom, the educational model switched from the humanities to theology, the focus of dominant attention switched from humanity to God. Theology became primary rather than secondary; it became the queen of the sciences. The axis moved from knowledge of humanity to knowledge of God. This is not to say that the humanities became unimportant. Their importance is clear, for example, in the thought of St Augustine. But they were now the supporting arches of knowledge rather than the key to knowledge, and the same is true of the natural sciences. As we saw earlier, Christian theology developed during the medieval period in an environment that contained no other religious traditions that were taken seriously. Theology was Christian and monolithic. Nevertheless within this theologically dominant model science and the humanities had their place. Like the Graeco–Roman *humanitas* model it was integral and unified. The difference was that *theologia* rather than the humanities provided the focal point of the model.

At the beginning of the modern period dominated by the rise of the West, John Locke was giving vent to this same intuition: that theology is the comprehension of all other knowledge, directed to its true end. It was in fact at the time of John Locke, and in the work of some of his own friends, that a new model began to emerge that was destined to dominate the educational scene up to our own day. This scientific model took a long time to flower. It seemed on occasion, through the Renaissance and the

Enlightenment, that *humanitas* was about to come back onto centre stage. Slowly but surely research into nature by means of the natural scientific method based upon induction, controlled experiment, number, prediction, objectivity, and practical application became the order of the day. The humanities and theology were persuaded, reluctantly or otherwise, to acquiesce in the new scheme of things. Methods suitable for application to nature were harnessed for application to humanity and even to God. At the same time the natural scientific model introduced another principle that made it different from *humanitas* and *theologia*. They had maintained the integrity of all knowledge at the same time as they had assumed that their own area of knowledge was slightly more equal than the others. The scientific model was based upon the pregnant notion that it is necessary to isolate particular problems for specialised solution. The assumption was that in order to advance knowledge it was necessary to split off areas of knowledge and to set up different disciplines that could go their own way. The scientific model is a fragmented rather than an integral one. It is not that the humanities and theology are subordinate parts of a greater whole. There no longer remains a wholistic view of what is knowledge? what is truth? what is a university? There is a crying need for a new integration of knowledge in order to speak to our global situation.

There is no space to pursue this point that is highlighted by *philosophia perennis*, alluded to by Wilfred Cantwell Smith, and covered elsewhere in my own writings.[28] What is crystal clear is that *philosophia perennis* pinpoints this dilemma and it is a crucial one in a book entitled *Christian theology and world religions: a global approach*. The solution that it offers is simple and twofold. It suggests on the one hand that the whole area of knowledge formerly confined to Christian theology should be widened to include other religions and that the spirituality element in theology should be given far deeper prominance so that transcendent Reality and the transcendent element in human nature can achieve the recognition they deserve. At this juncture *philosophia perennis* is clearly more part of Religious Studies than Christian theology. On the other hand it suggests that knowledge is integral and wholistic and yet at the same time it is hierarchical. Nature and the natural sciences matter but they are at a lower level than the humanities with their stress upon humanity and mind. The humanities matter more but they are at a lower level than religious studies which have a stake in the study of God and in the transcendent dimensions of soul and spirit.

(iv) Critique. Fourthly and finally let me offer a critique of the *philosophia perennis* solution to the topic that lies before us, for it will be obvious that my own thinking both converges with and diverges from that of this school.

It is clear that although the perennial philosophy overlaps with both Christian theology and Religious Studies it does not fit snugly into either. It is, so to speak, neither fish, meat, nor fowl and it is partly for this reason that it seems perplexing to scholars who are used to ordered disciplinary boundaries. However for this very reason it has much to offer to our discussion. For, together with the thought of Wilfred Cantwell Smith, it has already made a good contribution to global thinking at a time when Christian theology and Religious Studies in their more staid forms have been timid and defensive in face of this awesome task. In its stress upon God, transcendence, and spirituality it has blazed the trail for Christian theology and Religious Studies to follow. For, we may well ask, if they will not speak to these topics at a global level who will? Scholars in the humanities and natural sciences presumably will not! The perennial philosophy presents a challenge to both Christian theology and Religious Studies to rise above their more parochial concerns and become deeply involved in the cosmic and universal questions of our global situation.

However the concern of *philosophia perennis* for fours is less obviously relevant than the concentration upon threes we have experimented with in this book. My own thinking centres upon the three educational models we have looked at: the natural sciences, the humanities, and religious studies—and what appear to me to be the three human dimensions—the bodily, the mental, and the transcendental—and the three focal points of concern—nature, humanity, and transcendence. The perennial philosophy divides the third element into two so that transcendence becomes the manifest God and the unmanifest God, and the transcendent dimension within human nature becomes soul and spirit. The inference is that lying behind the natural sciences that deal with body and nature, the humanities that deal with humanity and mind, and religious studies and theology that deal with soul and the manifest God there lies the perennial philosophy that deals with spirit and the unmanifest God. This fourth element remains unconvincing. The other three form natural archetypes, the fourth does not.

Furthermore questions may be raised in regard to the emphasis of the perennial philosophy school upon hierarchy. There is an element of nostalgia in their work. They are attempting to return in a finessed way to the medieval hierarchy, to return the natural sciences to the relatively low role they had in that hierarchy, and to assert the supremacy of transcendence especially as seen through the spectacles of *philosophia perennis*. However hierarchy is not the only method of linking things. Different elements can be linked together without being graded as superior and inferior. They can be seen as complementary and different. If therefore nature, humanity and transcendence, and the bodily, mental and transcendent dimensions of human nature are different archetypes, they can be seen as complementary rather than 'in competition'. Thus if the supremacy of the natural sciences is slowly being modified this does not necessarily mean that the humanities or religious studies must again become supreme. The implication may simply be that these three areas and archetypes could become complementary and roughly equal.

Hierarchy can also be interpreted in another way within religious traditions themselves. We have already seen how *philosophia perennis* stresses spirituality. In fact the perennial philosophy can be interpreted as a kind of metaphysical spirituality, and the inference is that religious people can be graded according to the level of their spirituality. It is true, as we have said before, that Christian theology needs to give more attention to spirituality. However it remains within my model one element among eight that together make up a religious tradition. Some authentically religious persons gravitate naturally to the way of communal obedience, or worship, or love, or social involvement, or scriptural devotion, or thinking discipleship, or aesthetic sensitivity. The fact that they express their religiousness mainly through one of these ways rather than through overt spirituality does not of itself constitute them as inferior. It merely suggests that they are different. What matters is that they have a stake in transcendence and that it is *their* stake in transcendence. The salt of the earth and the citizens of the kingdom of heaven are not necessarily defined by spirituality even though they may possess it as one characteristic among others.

4. CONCLUSIONS

We have spent time upon the work of Wilfred Cantwell Smith and *philosophia perennis* because they add important elements to any discussion of Christian theology and world religions in a global age. Like Smith, the perennial philosophy ranges in wider pastures than those of Christian theology because it is concerned with all the religious traditions. Like Smith, it is not content to remain at the level of the social sciences and the humanities within the study of religion because it has a deep interest in transcendence. Unlike Smith, its curiosity is not aroused by theology in the sense of concepts and doctrines insofar as its deeper interest is in the metaphysics of comparative religion as seen through the spectrum of spirituality. To the extent that Smith and *philosophia perennis* are basically engaged in comparative religion they are closer to the milieu of Religious Studies than to that of Christian theology. Yet they are prophetic in relation to both. Their challenge to both is that they should become more involved in global issues. They should become involved not just at the level of the humanities—although this is important to determine what is the nature of humaneness in our global world; they should become involved not only at the level of nature—for this too is important in our age of ecological concern; they should become involved also at the level of transcendence—for this is a significant part of their proper concern. More than this, insofar as both (and especially Religious Studies) contain or bestraddle different areas of knowledge they can contribute towards the reintegration of knowledge and the reconnecting of separated elements of consciousness that will contribute to the forging of a new world.

FOOTNOTES

1. For further information on Smith see:– Introduction by Willard Oxtoby in *Religious diversity*, ed. Willard G Oxtoby, Crossroad, New York, new edition, 1982; Introduction by Frank Whaling in *The World's Religious Traditions: Current Perspectives in Religious Studies*, edited by Frank Whaling, T & T Clark, Edinburgh, 1984.

2. W C Smith, *'Comparative Religion: Whither and Why?'* in M Eliade and J Kitagawa, (eds), *The History of Religions: Essays in Methodology*, University of Chicago Press, Chicago, 1959, pp 31–58.

3. *Ibid*, p 58.

4. See F Whaling, *The World's Religious Traditions: Current Perspectives in Religious Studies*, T & T Clark, Edinburgh, 1984, pp 10–11.

5. W C Smith, *The Meaning and End of Religion*, New American Library, New York, 1964, p 16.

6. *Ibid*, p 48.

7. *Ibid*, p 141.

8. *Ibid*, p 141.

9. *Ibid*, p 141.

10. See W C Smith, *'A "Christian" Theology of Comparative Religion?'* in W C Smith, *Towards a World Theology*, Westminster Press, Philadelphia, 1981, pp 107–29.

11. The point about nouns and adjectives is picked up in W C Smith, *Questions of Religious Truth*, V Gollancz, London & Charles Scribner's Sons, New York, 1967; the point about humankind having one religious life is picked up in *'A History of Religion in the Singular'* in *Towards a World Theology*, Westminster Press, Philadelphia, 1981, pp 3–20.

12. W C Smith, *The Meaning and End of Religion*, New American Library, New York, 1964, p 17.

13. W C Smith, *Questions of Religious Truth*, V Gollancz Ltd., London & Charles Scribner's sons, New York, 1967, p 36.

14. W C Smith, *Towards a World Theology*, Westminster Press, Philadelphia, 1981, p 193: 'One might urge "from dialogue to colloquy" as a slogan within the Church.'

15. Huston Smith, *Forgotten Truth: the Primordial Tradition*, Harper &

Row, New York, 1975; Huston Smith, 'Perennial Philosophy, Primordial Tradition' in Huston Smith, *Beyond the Post-Modern Mind*, Crossroad, New York, 1982; Seyyed Hossein Nasr, *Knowledge and The Sacred*, Edinburgh University Press, Edinburgh, 1981; S H Nasr, 'The Philosophia Perennis and the Study of Religion' in F Whaling, (ed), *The World's Religious Traditions: Current Perspectives in Religious Studies*, T & T Clark, Edinburgh, 1984, pp 181–200.

16. See F Whaling, *Contemporary Approaches to the Study of Religion*, Volume One, *The Humanities*, Mouton, Berlin New York Amsterdam, 1984, pp 397–401 on Coomaraswamy, pp 413–416 on Nasr.

17. Aldous Huxley, *The Perennial Philosophy*, Harper and Brothers, New York, 1945, p vii.

18. S H Nasr, p 193 in F Whaling, (ed), *The World's Religious Traditions: Current Perspectives in Religious Studies*, T & T Clark, Edinburgh, 1984.

19. *Ibid*, p 187.

20. Huston Smith, *Beyond the Post-Modern Mind*, Crossroad, New York, 1982, p 52.

21. *Ibid*, p 53.

22. S H Nasr, p 192 in F Whaling, (ed), *The World's Religious Traditions: Current Perspectives in Religious Studies*, T & T Clark, Edinburgh, 1984.

23. The Paulist Press, Ramsey N. J., conceptualised *The Classics of Western Spirituality* which is now two-thirds complete. It contains up-to-date translations, editions and presentations of what will eventually be seventy classics of western spirituality by internationally recognised scholars. The classics are mainly Christian but include also some Jewish, Muslim and American Indian volumes.

24. *World Spirituality: an Encyclopaedic History of the Religious Quest* is projected in twenty-six volumes by the Crossroad Press, New York, to present the spirituality of all the religious traditions of the world.

25. See *The Limits to Growth: a Report for the Club of Rome's Project on the Predicament of Mankind*, Pan Books, London and Sydney, 1974.

26. See Ervin Laszlo, *The Inner Limits of Mankind*, Pergamon, Oxford, 1978.

27. See Willis W Harman, 'The "Global Premises" Project', pp. II.71–75, in *Forum*, 11:4, March 1981.

28. See F Whaling, '*The Study of Religion in a Global Context*', pp 391–451, in F Whaling (ed), *Contemporary Approaches to the Study of Religion*, Volume One, *The Humanities*, Mouton, Berlin New York Amsterdam, 1984; F Whaling, 'Towards a New Integration', in *Forum* (9) pp 59–70 & (10) pp 46–57, 1979.

CHAPTER SIX

THE RENEWING OF CHRISTIAN THEOLOGY THROUGH WORLD RELIGIONS

1. DIFFERENCES BETWEEN CHRISTIAN THEOLOGY AND RELIGIOUS STUDIES

The time has come for us to leave the profitable byways of our last chapter and return to the task of Christian theology as such. In the preceding pages we saw by implication that Christian theology overlaps with but is different from Religious Studies. Let us pause for a moment to rehearse these differences before passing on to see how Christian theology can be renewed through its contact with world religions. It is clear that this survey must be brief insofar as, as is obvious from our previous discussion, there is no universal consensus as to what is the exact nature of either Christian theology or Religious Studies. An implied analysis of both is contained in this book and we pause now to compare the main contours of these two important areas of thought.

The obvious difference is that Christian theology is basically particular. It has to do with a particular religious tradition. Any wider statements it has to make, as we saw in our discussion of the Christian approaches to other religious traditions, arise out of a starting-point within Christianity. Christian theology, therefore, is basically the theology arising out of the Christian tradition. Religious Studies, on the other hand, includes within its orbit a study of all the religious traditions of the world. It is not confined to the study of one, nor does it use the categories of one tradition to interpret all the others. Its concern is for all.

Another obvious difference lies in the use of the word 'theology'. The proper realm of theology is that of the science or knowledge of God. God or transcendence are central to the concerns of theology because the very word itself has to do with *theos*, God. If theology chooses *not* to concern itself with Ultimate Reality, legitimate questions can be asked and explanations are in order. Religious Studies, by contrast, is involved more in the study of religious data and in the religiousness of human beings. It is concerned to chart the history of different religious traditions and to explore the manifold data of religious traditions. It is concerned also to examine the intentions and the faith of believers. However its primary interest lies in the human side rather than the divine side of the religious equation. That which believers respond to, the object of their faith, is not the direct concern of Religious Studies. The religious dimension of human beings rather than Ultimate Reality as such is the legitimate concern of Religious Studies.

A further difference lies in the range and nuance of methods used in Christian theology and Religious Studies. We saw earlier how Christian theology has traditionally stressed doctrine. *Theologia* referred, at an early period in the development of Christian theology, to the doctrine of the Trinity. In the course of time it came to envelop doctrines about other matters, earlier known as *oikonomia*, so that it covered Christian doctrine in general. It is of course true to say that Christian theology can have, in certain contexts, a wider meaning so that it comes to include, as well as systematic theology, the other areas in my model such as the history of the Christian churches, Christian liturgy, Christian ethics, Christian social and political involvement, Biblical studies, Christian aesthetics, and Christian spirituality. However doctrine (and to a lesser extent spirituality) has held a certain primacy. Right belief has mattered to Christians. The fact of belief has been stressed by Christians more than others. Therefore Christian theology has, during the course of its development, become naturally and intrinsically engaged in the exposition, defence, and interpretation of Christian doctrine. The conceptual bent has been to the fore. Religious Studies, in comparison, has given at least equal weight to non-doctrinal considerations. It has been concerned with the history of religious traditions, the anthropological study of myths, rituals and symbols, the philological study of texts, the sociological study of religious groups, the phenomenological study of religious experience, the psychological study of religious mysticism, and the aesthetic study of religious art, as well as the investigation of religious doctrines. Moreover in intention it has studied these matters comparatively as well as within particular religious traditions. By comparison, therefore, with Christian theology, Religious Studies has had a less particular stress upon one specific tradition namely Christianity, a less particular stress upon one specific approach namely theology, a less particular stress upon a specific element in religion namely the conceptual, and a less particular stress upon the transcendent object of religion namely Ultimate Reality. As we saw in the last chapter it is not quite as simple as this in that Wilfred Cantwell Smith and *philosophia perennis* operate on the borders between Christian theology and Religious Studies—they stress transcendence and conceptual matters from a stance located within Religious Studies rather than Christian theology. Nevertheless, although there will always be overlap between the two areas it is useful to delimit the differences between them. In this way they can complement one another. When we raise the more particular question of how can Christian theology learn from world religions we are encroaching upon the wider question of how can Christian theology learn from Religious Studies (and vice versa).

2. RENEWAL OF CHRISTIAN THEOLOGY BY 'PASSING OVER' INTO OTHER RELIGIONS

However we must now concentrate upon the straight question of how Christian theology can renew itself through its contact with world religions. Before we home in upon this question exclusively we must first of all raise the 'how' matter more existentially. For readers in the continents of Africa and Asia there is likely to be little dilemma for they will have easy contact with members of other religions. For western readers, in spite of the immigration of believers from other cultures and easier travel, the solution may be not so straightforward.

For their benefit we recommend the spiritual technique of 'passing-over' that we will now describe.

We presuppose that the student has already done some spadework on other religions on the lines laid out in chapter two. It would be ludicrous to imagine that it is possible to pass over into another religious tradition without having some knowledge of it. Having some knowledge of other religions is however a preliminary to passing over into an empathetic awareness of the faith of other humans. To know the religion of another is more than being cognisant of the facts of the other's religious tradition. It involves getting inside the skin of the other, it involves walking in the other's shoes, it involves seeing the world in some sense as the other sees it, it involves asking the other's questions, it involves getting inside the other's sense of 'being a Hindu, Muslim, Jew, Buddhist, or whatever'. We saw earlier that the theological approach of dialogue may involve some of these qualities. 'Passing over' may involve dialogue. On the other hand it may not. It is unlikely that it can be accomplished without some occasional contact with the practitioners of the other religion, but the dedicated intention to penetrate the world-view of another through imaginative feats of empathy can be effective. The difference from dialogue is that passing over has the theological motive of renewing one's own theological insight by getting inside the theological consciousness of another. As well as, or instead of, the motive of making significant contact with the other that is involved in dialogue there is the realis- ation that passing over into the world-view of another is a significant touchstone for Christian theological renewal. For passing over involves returning again theologically renewed by contact with the other. There is a sense in which medieval theologians such as Aquinas passed over into the world-view of Aristotle. They did not engage in actual dialogue with Aristotle for he was long dead but they did get inside the world-view he represented and, having done that, they returned to renew their own theological world. The present- day challenge and opportunity is to pass over into the world- view of other cultures either by actual dialogue or by concep- tual engagement.

John Dunne has explored the process of 'passing over' in a slightly different context. As he puts it:

> The holy man of our time, it seems, is not a figure like Gotama or Jesus or Mohammed, a man who could found a world religion, but a figure like Gandhi, a man who passes over by sympathetic understanding from his own religion to other religions and comes back again with new insight to his own. Passing over and coming back, it seems, is the spiritual adventure of our time ... It starts from the homeland of a man's own religion, goes through the wonderland of other religions, and ends in the homeland of his own.[1]

Dunne is talking about a personal spiritual odyssey. It is our contention that a similar process can be applied to the odyssey of theological renewal. The 'how' then of renewing Christian theology by contact with other traditions is that of 'passing over' and 'return'.

There is not the space to catalogue the myriad of instances of theological renewal that are beginning to occur in our day through the Christian contact with other religions. There are so many examples, and they relate to many different areas of theology, that it is difficult to choose the ones that are most relevant for our purpose. In order to avoid arbitrariness, I intend to use instances from my own recent experience in Africa and China. These examples have the added advantage that they diverge from the major religious traditions that we have stressed so far and open up sources of renewal from less well known areas of the religious world.

3. RENEWAL OF CHRISTIAN THEOLOGY THROUGH AFRICAN RELIGION

In the summer of 1984 I had the opportunity to lecture on African Religion in southern Africa. This gave me contact with the mainstream Christian churches in southern Africa, with some of the indigenous African churches in that region, and with some of the African traditional religions that are situated there. Especially in the case of the African traditional religions and their indigenised adaptation by the African indigenous churches there was real sense of 'passing over' into an African world view. The 'return' from that world-view opened up creative insights into elements of Christian theology that had been dormant for me before that visit.[2]

(a) Communion of Saints. In the first place it renewed my thinking about the meaning of the phrase 'the communion of saints'. In the Roman Catholic Church the tendency has been to equate saints with special people, and in other mainstream churches the tendency has been to pay lipservice to Christians who have passed on—in existential and liturgical practice they are largely forgotten. Africans have a strong tradition of living in relationship with the living-dead or the ancestors. There is a continuity of life between the living, the living-dead, and the yet-to-be-born. The ancestors join in the prayers of the living, and they are present in worship. They speak, as it were, of a continuity between the Church Militant and the Church Triumphant. Worship includes not only those who are physically present in a service; the living-dead, the saints, are also present in the praise and rejoicing. Christians have a greater sense of continuity between past and present; the saints are present watching over us and encouraging us.[3]

(b) God, Humanity and Nature. In the second place being in Africa led to renewed thinking about our co-creativity with God over nature, allied to an increasing sense of the integral relations of humanity with the earth. In western theology, Genesis set up a hierarchy whereby God created the earth, God created humanity in his own image, and God gave humanity dominion over the earth. This hierarchy had the potentiality of becoming graded so that human beings could become distant from the earth to the extent that subduing the earth could be turned into exploiting the earth. Africans have managed to retain their art of communion with the earth while co-creating the world with God. For them there is a more natural proclivity to think in terms of the inter-relation-ships between God, humanity and the earth so that they are seen as a complementary hierarchy rather than a sundered one. This reintegration within theological consciousness of

God, humanity and nature is a valuable African contribution to the renewal of Christian theology.[4]

(c) Symbols, dreams and visions. In the third place, Africa has an intrinsic interest in symbolism and this fuels the revival of interest in symbolism in Christian theology today. African traditional religions, and through them increasingly Christians in Africa, retain an interest in symbols, dreams and visions. There is a sense in Africa of interior communion with the archetypal world of one's own consciousness. Africans point out that the Bible contains a lot about symbols, dreams and visions. They show how ministers are often called to the ministry through some sort of vision. The western theological stress, by contrast, has stressed reason, the individual, science, and so on, and has drawn us away from the archetypal world of the unconscious and away from the world of symbolism. The result tends to be that the symbols are less insistent, we are less able to intuit the sacred, and we are drawn away from our inner selves. It is perhaps no accident that, through van der Post and others, Carl Jung and Africa are being linked. We are beginning to refind theologically symbols, dreams and visions; we are witnessing a renewal of theological symbolism.[5]

(d) Religious healing. A fourth area of African prodding to theological reflection lies in the realm of religious healing. The African Independent Churches have always stressed that Jesus spent much time in healing the sick, and that healing equals wholeness. This fuels the growing awareness within the wider church of the relationship between medicine and theology, and of the psychosomatic roots of much illness.[6]

(e) Initiation and death. A fifth area of interest is the importance of *rites de passage*, especially initiation and death. I was privileged to be present at the initiation of an *izangoma* at Soweto, and at various funeral services, and it was clear how significant they were. Victor Turner the anthropologist talks about the state of liminality present in initiation and death which involve a critically important passage from one state of life to another. This contrasts with the low-key nature of much western treatment of initiation and death. Africans take

them very seriously indeed, and this seriousness is important for wider theological reflection.[7]

(f) *Church as community.* Sixthly it appeared to me that there are implications for Christian theology in the African emphasis upon 'man-in-community'. The African insight is that we find our full personality in group relations rather than in individual isolation. To this extent, the Body of Christ, the Church, is more theologically vital to Africans. The Church is not a random coming-together of individuals. It is inherently a sense of belonging. It involves a sense of responsibility to the community, as well as a sense of freedom in the community.[8]

(g) *The good life.* Finally the African stress is less upon material goods for their own sake. The good life is not equated with luxuries. There is a greater stress upon inter-personal relationships, humanity, life, and the sharing of life. There is a sense that personal values matter more than mechanical expertise and that they must be preserved in a global techno-logical world. This stress upon 'life' rather than 'things' is another instance of the slant that Africa is beginning to give to Christian theology.[9]

My sense of passing-over into the world-view of African religion was deeper than can be explored here. The same is true of the sense of theological renewal upon return. The Christian theological riches to be found in Africa are vast; they are already being mined; and their finest veins are still to be explored. Their potentiality is obvious and, while visits like the one I made are important, their realisation is not solely dependent upon living in Africa. The work of the African Church and dedicated conceptual passing-over have their part to play.[10]

4. RENEWAL OF CHRISTIAN THEOLOGY THROUGH CHINESE WORLD-VIEWS

(a) *Background.* Our second example is taken from China and it was in the summer of 1982 that I was able to visit China as an exchange Fellow of the British Academy. In the People's

Republic of China I met the leaders of the Catholic, Christian (equals Protestant), Buddhist, and Muslim traditions in China; I visited many Buddhist temples, Muslim mosques, and Catholic and Christian churches; and I had the sense of passing-over into the Chinese Christian world-view and to some extent the Chinese world-view.

It was a moving experience but it was an experience on a different level from that in Africa. Southern Africa had been a capitalist and white-dominated society, China was socialist and non-white; the Christian tradition had been dominant in southern Africa, in China it was a small minority; the main partner in renewal in Africa had been African primal religion, in China primal religion was viewed as 'superstition' and only the major religions were actively tolerated; in Africa the theological structure of an often remote High God and intermediate spirits in touch with human needs was not too dissimilar from that of God the Father and God the Son, in China there was an utterly different world-view; in Africa the touchstones for renewal had been religious in a more conventional sense, in China a quasi-religious force namely Marxism was of at least equal importance as a spur to renewal.

My port of entry into China was inevitably Hong Kong, and in Hong Kong I stayed at a Christian Ecumenical Centre that symbolised the whole process of passing-over. Its Chinese name is Tao Fong Shan. Its insignia is a cross rising out of a lotus—key Christian and Buddhist emblems passing-over into and returning from each other. Its original guiding spirit was Karl Reichelt who had arrived in China in 1903. He felt called to pass-over into Chinese Buddhism and Taoism, and to allow Chinese Buddhists and Taoists to pass-over into Christianity. In 1927 he moved his sphere of operations from Nanking to Hong Kong, and Tao Fong Shan (the Mountain where the Wind of the Tao Blows) came into being as a 'passing-over centre'. In that same year 1927 Logan Roots wrote in a preface to Reichelt's *Truth and tradition in Chinese Buddhism*:

I believe we can hardly fail to see from this study, even if we have not seen it before, that deeper knowledge of its own surpassing inheritance will come to Christianity from such intercourse as this book records and invites between itself and Buddhism.[11]

Through the work of Reichelt, and through the work of Tao Fong Shan and places like it, Christians have passed-over into Buddhism and returned from it with theological fruits that already show promise of an abundant harvest. However my own pilgrimage was not so much into the world-view of Chinese Buddhism as into the world-view of the new China. When I took the plane from Hong Kong to Beijing, I was moving into a vastly different world from that of Tao Fong Shan and essaying a different theological task from that of Karl Reichelt. For the sake of succinctness we will concentrate upon my own experience in mainland China rather than the crucially important venture of passing-over into Buddhism. We will concentrate also upon my passing-over into the Chinese Christians' passing-over into the new China.

(b) In the world but not of it. The Chinese Christians are giving new meaning to the phrase 'living in the world yet not of the world'. They are triumphantly in the world as never before. They are part, an enthusiastic part, of the new China. They see the church as incarnate in China, not separate from it as was once the case. They look with amused tolerance upon liberation theologies in the churches of other lands. For them, liberation in the sense of the removal of unnecessary poverty and injustice has already occurred in China. It occurred partly through politics, and partly through a continuation of earlier religious themes such as the Confucian faith in the meaningfulness of humanity. The Chinese Christians have passed-over into the communist ethos, and also into the Confucian notion that being religious is 'being engaged in ultimate self-transformation as a communal act'.[12] Having returned from the passing-over process they are aware that grace elevates nature rather than supercedes it. They see God's prevenient grace at work in all persons including (perhaps especially) their communist neighbours. Their themes are reconciliation rather than confrontation, identification rather than separation, evolving hope rather than esch-

atological millennium, and the incarnation, death and resurrection of Christ as relevant not only to the church but also to China herself.

(c) Transcendence. Yet, in spite of this intense identification with their environment, the Chinese Christians are also aware that their belief in God is at odds with atheism however warmly they may regard the praxis that has transformed China. While being strongly committed to their neighbours in the arena of service and daily life, their faith remains in the transcendent God. And it is in grappling with this theme of transcendence, a theme strangely neglected within much western theology, that Chinese Christian theology has much to teach us. For Chinese Christian theologians, transcendence is not merely an interesting concept that Christians may wish to examine. It is Ultimate Reality which gives point to everything else. Yet this same Ultimate Reality, this same transcendence that differentiates us from our neighbour in a profound way, also reconciles us with our neighbour, also pervades the profane, and also motivates the service whereby we are led, so to speak, to wash our neighbour's feet. I suspect that it is above all in relation to this theme of transcendence that we have much to learn from Chinese Christians. Part of the lesson is that we do not have to conform to our world theologically (the Chinese view of transcendence whether it be communist historical inevitability, Confucian Heaven or Taoist Way has never been obtrusive)[13] in order to be the humane leaven in it.

(d) Prayer and Spirituality. Another Chinese touchstone for renewal is quite simply the importance of prayer and spirituality. In face of flux and uncertainty in the external world, sources of courage have been tapped in the spiritual world. There has been no guarantee that the present relatively safe haven would be reached. Leadership has been removed at key traumatic occasions. Questions of conscience to which there have been no certain answer have been present all along. In the midst of all this, the churches have grown. Through spiritual adaptation the Chinese Christians have managed not only to survive but also to increase. Almost by accident, through the house churches, Chinese Christians

have discovered the importance in Christian spirituality of *koinonia*, small group fellowship. They have also discovered the importance of praying for one another. Wherever I went the plea was 'when you return to your land ask the Christians there to pray for us'. This was not just a polite negative to potential offers of money, personnel, or material goods—it was a positive thirst for the spiritual help that prayer affords. Chinese Christians have also discovered, again sometimes by chance—for example by exile into the countryside during the Cultural Revolution—the spiritual solace to be found through nature. The Taoist and Ch'an (Zen) Buddhist feel for nature as mirroring the spiritual nature within has found an answering chord in the Christian soul.[14] In all these ways prayer and spirituality have become heightened in the Chinese Christian experience and as such they speak to us.

(e) Christian and wider ecumenism. The Chinese Christians have also experimented ecumenically. The Protestants have united to form the Christian Church. Former Methodists I met were occasionally aware of my own work on the Wesleys but were not nostalgic for a lost Methodist paradise. They were happy to be united with other Christians. The extraordinary plethora of former Chinese churches was an unlamented relic of the past. Curiously the Roman Catholic Church remains alongside the Christian Church as a separate Christian way. This seemed strange until one realised that this dual Christian presence could be seen within the Chinese imagery of *yin* and *yang*.[15] *Yin* and *yang* are different but they complement one another. Like male and female, valley and mountain, black and white, they form a dualism of contrasts. And yet there is a sense in which they need each other and stand in relation to each other. They are not opposing armies but complementary parts of a wider whole. At a wider ecumenical level there are friendly relations between Catholics, Protestant Christians, Buddhists, Muslims and people of all religions. This situation of friendship and dialogue has been promoted by the dialectic of the Chinese experience. That experience is exemplary in the case of the Confucians, Taoists and Buddhists who had formed the *San Chiao*, the three intermingling ways, of Chinese Religion; it is persuasive in the case of the Chinese commu-

nists who preferred a tidy religious situation to deal with. In either case, in regard to Christian ecumenism or inter-religious ecumenism, the Chinese pattern is instructive.

(f) Transcendence, humanity and nature. A final spur to renewal emanating from China may be even more important. It repeats with a different nuance a similar theme important in Africa. It focuses upon the inter-relationship between transcendence, humanity, and nature. This inter-communion between heaven, human beings, and earth has been a leitmotif of Confucian thought,[16] It dates back before the time of Christ to the Book of History, and it was developed noticeably in classical Confucianism. As the Book of Ritual puts it, humanity is 'the understanding heart of Heaven and earth'.[17] Christians in China have inherited this sense of the complementary relationships between Heaven, earth, and persons. Anyone who has seen the sheer beauty of a Taoist centre, with natural and human handiworks intertwining with each other, or a thousand and one other examples of the Chinese feel for nature will recognise that nature and humanity have not known dislocation in China. Equally the history of Chinese philosophy and religion is pervaded by the search, the persistent and sometimes desperate search, for a meaningful human society. As Mencius put it, 'when love and righteousness are thwarted, beasts will be led to devour men and men will devour each other'.[18] If rulers ignore the Mandate of Heaven to build a caring society, it is likely that their mandate will be taken away from them, and there are those in China today who are able to apply the notion of the Mandate of Heaven to the communist takeover. Less emphasised has been the third element in the equation, namely transcendence or Heaven. With its stress upon transcendence that we noted above, Chinese Christian theology is in a position to reintegrate for China and for Christian theology the inter-connecting elements of transcendence, humanity, and nature. By giving new value to transcendence, by accepting the communist gloss upon the Confucian concern for humanity, and by showing a proper concern for nature in the tradition of the Taoists and Zen Buddhists, Chinese Christians are in the vanguard of Christian passing-

over into the Chinese sense of the inter-communion between the constituent elements of all existence—transcendence, humanity, and nature. My own passing-over into China and Chinese Christianity brought me back with an urgent sense of the importance for Christians everywhere of immediate Christian theological wrestling with this fundamental question.

5. IMPORTANCE OF PASSING-OVER FOR CHRISTIAN THEOLOGY

It would be possible to pile up many other examples of Christian theological passing-over into and returning from other cultural and religious traditions, for example from my four-year stay in India or from my more superficial contact with American Indians. However, as we saw earlier, actual travel to another culture, although desirable, is not essential in order to engage in theological renewal through other religions. Knowledge of another religion, empathy with it, and the realisation that theological enhancement can be obtained from it—all these provide the motivating tools for passing-over into and returning from other religious traditions. Passing-over on its own is not sufficient. The American Indians say that in order truly to understand another person one must first walk for a mile in that person's moccasins. To gain theologically, it is necessary not only to walk in the other's moccasins but also to return with that moccasin experience and to conceptualise it into Christian theology. Through imaginative use of the mind and spirit we can leave our own world, our own context, our own religious tradition and we can enter into the faith and tradition of others. So renewed, we can return to our world, our context, and our religious tradition with a new outlook and vision that can be turned into theoligical capital. For Christian theology, to be truly global is to utilise the world-views of all the great cultures so that Christian theology can become universal and global. No longer imprisoned within the thought-world of the West, no longer constrained by cultural boundaries, the Christian theology of the future will be able to address itself to global consciousness in the knowledge that only sin can separate us from the love of God in Christ. Factors that in the world's parochial past were held to separate the Christian from his or her Source, located in the culture, language, religion or sheer strangeness of others, are transmuted from symbols of confrontation into the negative plates of renewal whereby Christian theology can speak to global needs.

6. WORLD RELIGIONS AND THE FUTURE OF CHRISTIAN THEOLOGY

As we said in the introduction, this is a time of theological pluralism in the Christian world. Indigenous Christian theology from Africa, Asia, and South America is mingling with Christian theological renewal movements within the western world. 'Passing-over and return' theology is mingling with secularisation, liberation, and process theology with their roots in the West. The Christian theological scene is both exciting and chaotic. There is neither the space nor the need to catalogue again the elements of this delicious theological chaos. In the affairs of theology as well as in the affairs of mortals there are times and tides, there are ebbs and flows. The present pluralism and change will give rise to future order; the present bewildering variety will give rise to a future system. Then doubtless that future order and system will be succeeded by another wave of theological ferment and see-sawing. The point is that the future of Christian theology—in its present semi-confusion, in the more organised systematic theology that will surely follow in the twenty-first century, and in the diversification that will doubtless succeed that system—will be integrally linked with the engagement with world religions we have described in this book. Indeed we have ventured to suggest that for Christian theology to have any future in a nuclear global world is partly contingent upon western Christian theology and the western world taking seriously and acting upon insights from other world-views. The other religious traditions of the world are not an optional extra in the process of Christian theological dialogue, they are not merely one partner among many others in the process of dialogue, they are the key factor whereby Christian theology can become truly global in a global world.

We have indicated in this chapter some of the insights for theological renewal emerging out of Africa and China. Had there been more space we could have done the same in regard to the Christian theological engagement with the major religions traditions of Islam, Judaism, Hinduism and Buddhism. Time is too short, and in any case the purpose of this book is more to whet the appetite than to encompass the whole task. In our final chapter we will look more closely at the impact of a particular tradition, that of the Hindus, upon a central Christian doctrine, that of the Trinity. In the meantime we hope that we have challenged the reader to set up a new vision of Christian theology in its relationships with other religions. No person, no culture, no religious tradition, no theology can remain an island. The world is our Christian theological parish. The Christian theological challenge is to think globally or perish—to perish if not through holocaust then through lack of the vision that feels true compassion for the whole of humankind. We trust that, in the pages of this book, we have called a new theological dialogue into being—with the other religious traditions of the world—to redress the balance of the old dialogue—with the secular forces of the West. Both dialogues are necessary. On balance, as I suspect we have shown, the engagement with world religions is of deeper import. For it opens up global possibilities for Christian theology not only in the geographical world of our revolving sphere but also in the psychological world of our human nature which knows that secular concerns are only part of the whole that makes us free.

FOOTNOTES

1. John S Dunne, *The Way of all the Earth*, University of Notre Dame Press, Notre Dame, Indiana, 1978, p ix.
2. Inevitably what follows contains much personal observation and conversational reflection. Good general works on African Religion are:– John S Mbiti, *African Religions and Philosophy*, Doubleday & Co., New York, 1970; Geoffrey Parrinder, *Religion in Africa*, Penguin, Harmondsworth, 1969; T O Ranger and I N Kimambo, *The Historical Study of African Religion*,

University of California Press, Berkeley, 1972; Benjamin C Ray, *African Religions*, Prentice-Hall, Englewood Cliffs N. J., 1976; N S Booth, (ed), *African Religions*, NOK Publishers, New York, 1977.

3. An early but influential western study of ancestors was G Parrinder, *African Traditional Religion*, Hutchinson's University Library, London, 1954, especially chapter five.

4. Lynn T White, *Frontiers of Knowledge in the Study of Man*, Harper, New York, 1956—and in other works—has been influential in his analysis of the possibly disruptive implications of the Genesis structuring of God, humanity, and nature.

5. See B G M Sundkler, *Bantu Prophets in South Africa*, second edition, Oxford University Press, London, 1961; Laurens van der Post, *Jung and the Story of our Time*, Penguin, Harmondsworth, 1978.

6. See M L Daniel, *Zionism and Faith Healing in Rhodesia*, Mouton, The Hague, 1970.

7. Victor W Turner, *The Ritual Process*, Aldine Pub. Co., Chicago, 1969; *Drums of Affliction*, Oxford University Press, London, 1968; *Forest of Symbols*, Cornell University Press, Ithaca, 1967.

8. This is brought out in John V Taylor, *The Primal Vision*, SCM Press, London, 1963.

9. See Placide Tempels, *Bantu Philosophy*, Présence Africaine, Paris, 1959.

10. Helpful books on Christian theology in Africa are:– Malcolm J McVeigh, *God in Africa*, Claude Stark Inc., Cape Cod, 1974; Aylward Shorter, *African Christian Theology*, Orbis, Maryknoll, 1977; K. Appiah-Kubi and S Torres, *African Theology en Route*, Orbis, Maryknoll, 1981; John S Mbiti, *Concepts of God in Africa*, SPCK, London, 1970; Aylward Shorter, *Prayer in the Religious Traditions of Africa*, Oxford University Press, London, 1975. I am deeply grateful to various *izangomas* of African traditional religions, leaders of African indigenous churches, and Christians of all races from many different mainstream churches through whom I was able to pass over into African religion and return renewed in life and theology.

11. Karl Reichelt, *Truth and Tradition in Chinese Buddhism*, second edition, Paragon Book Reprint, New York, 1969.

12. Tu Wei-Ming, 'A Confucian Perspective in Learning to be Human' p 70, in F Whaling, (ed) *The World's Religious Traditions: Current Perspecticves in Religious Studies*, (T and T Clark, Edinburgh, 1984).

13. See C Larre, '*The Meaning of Transcendence in Chinese Thought*' pp 42–51 in *China as a Challenge to the Church*, edited by C Geffré and J Spae, Seabury Press, New York, 1979.

14. See for example William Johnston, *The Still Point, Reflections on Zen and Christian Mysticism*, Fordham University Press, New York, 1977.

15. W C Smith, *The Faith of Other Men*, New American Library, New York, 1965, pp 63–75; H Wilhelm, *Change, Eight Lectures on the I Ching*, Harper & Row, New York, 1960; F Capra, *The Tao of Physics*, Wildwood House, London, 1975.

16. See Thomas Berry, 'Affectivity in Classical Confucian Tradition' pp 1–29 in T Berry (ed.), *Riverdale Papers III*, Riverdale Center, New York, n.d.

17. *Book of Ritual* 7:3: text from S. Courvreur, *Memoires Sur Les Bienseances et Les Ceremonies*, Paris, 1950.

18. *Mencius* 3B:9; ed. J Legge, *The Chinese Classics*, Oxford University Press, 1893.

CHAPTER SEVEN

INDIAN RELIGION AND THE CHRISTIAN DOCTRINE OF THE TRINITY

I. INTRODUCTION

Throughout this work, we have stressed that theology is primarily to do with God and with doctrine. It is therefore appropriate that in this final chapter we isolate the Christian doctrine of God the Trinity for discussion. We will investigate how the doctrine of the Trinity has been enlarged and deepened through the dialogue of Christian theology with Indian religion.

Our discussion will be in two stages. In the first place we will analyse the contribution made by Indian Christian theology to a global Christian theology of the Trinity. Indian Christian theologians have shed new conceptual light upon the doctrine of the Trinity by means of their dialogue with the Hindu tradition. They have also pointed out in a unique way that the fact that Christians think of God in terms of a Trinity has far-reaching implications for the Christian life itself. In this section we will rely to a large extent upon Indian Christian theology in order to show how Christian theology is being renewed through its engagement with Indian religion.

In the second stage we will go beyond Indian Christian theology as such in order to investigate how the Indian intuition that God is female as well as male can be meaningfully incorporated into the Christian doctrine of the Trinity. Globally the time is ripe for this theological leap. Attempts to feminise the masculine Trinity have not been notably successful. By extrapolation from Hindu thought, another approach suggests itself that may bear more fruit.

Our hope is that by focusing more minutely upon one doctrine and upon one other religious tradition, clues may be given that will be helpful in renewing our understanding of other Christian doctrines through creative contact with other religions.

2. INDIAN CHRISTIAN THEOLOGY AND THE TRINITY

(a) Background. Raja Ram Mohan Roy was attracted by Christian ideas at the end of the eighteenth century. He has been called the 'father of the Indian Renaissance' and he and his Hindu successors were profoundly influenced by Christian notions[1]. It is virtually impossible adequately to understand modern Hindu thought without taking seriously the effect upon it of Christian and western views. We are now beginning to realise that the converse is also the case. Indian Christian theologians have been influenced by the Hindu background within which they were thinking, living and writing[2]. In attempting to communicate the Gospel within this background, in attempting to express Christian truths in Indian terms, in attempting to conceptualise the Gospel in ways that would make sense to the thought-world of India, Indian Christians have begun to make exciting new contributions to world theology. In this chapter we are concerned with the contribution they have made in regard to the Trinity and the religious life arising from an Indian Christian view of the Trinity. A number of Indian Christian theologians have lent their talents to this new theological work and rather than concentrate upon one of them we will interpret the views of a number of these thinkers in order to gain an integral picture.

Western Christians have tended to isolate the doctrine of the Trinity from the rest of Christian doctrine and indeed from the practical living of the Christian life itself. Indeed the very word 'theology' does not figure in the New Testament and when it did begin to be used in the Patristic period it was sometimes isolated to refer solely to the doctrine of the Trinity. As we have seen, another word, namely *oikonomia* was used for doctrines of salvation and so on, and *theologia* was restricted among some of the Fathers to the doctrine of God in himself as a Trinity. This is not to say that the doctrine of the Trinity was not important or that it was completely isolated from other doctrine or from life. I am, however, suggesting that it was not fully bound up with wider doctrine and with life. This is not the case as far as Indian Christian theology is concerned. Indian theologians have made contributions to the doctrine of the Trinity and at the same time to practical theology as well. The two are bound together, and we must look at both.

In the first place it is worth making the obvious comment that the concept of the Trinity is important to them. As far as they are concerned God is not merely Christ, although he is certainly that; he is Father, Son, and Holy Spirit. They do not restrict God to Christ by indulging in a form of Christolatry. They recognise that the trinitarian nature of God is vital to Christian belief and life.

In the second place we may say that there is little possibility of Christian notions of the Trinity being aided either in theory or in practice by Christian contact with Jewish or Muslim world views insofar as they deny the concept of the Trinity. The same applies to Theravada Buddhist, Confucian and Taoist thought which equally have no doctrine of the Trinity. Mahayana Buddhist views of the Three Bodies of the Buddha seem to have superficial similarity to the Trinity with their reference to the Buddha in his historical aspect, in his glorified aspect, and in his cosmic aspect. However, this seeming resemblance turns out on closer examination to be a radical difference. Within the Hindu context Mathothu has written as a Christian upon the Hindu concept of the *trimurti*, the trinity of personal deities, namely Brahma the Creator, Vishnu the Preserver, and Shiva the Destroyer[3]. However, there seems to be little affinity between the *trimurti* and the Christian Trinity[4]. More promising ground exists within Indian thought in the concept of *Brahman*, Ultimate Reality, as capable of being expressed in a triune way, as also in the idea that Brahman is both without qualities (*nirguna*) and with qualities (*saguna*). Indian Christians have availed themselves of these concepts in order to give deeper meaning to the doctrine of the Trinity. Let us examine briefly how they have done this.

(b) The Trinity and Saccidananda. Classical Hindu thought had
suggested that the Absolute, Brahman, could be thought of
as *Saccidananda*, that is, *Sat, Cit,* and *Ananda*[5]. These three
terms mean Being, Intelligence and Bliss. They provided to
Indian Christian thinkers not merely an opportunity to
present Christ to Hindus in their own thought-patterns but
also the possibility of using these terms to deepen the meaning
of the Trinity for Christians. For Being could refer to God in
his ineffable aspect, Intelligence could refer to Christ as the
Logos, and Bliss could refer to the Holy Spirit who is the
Giver of Joy. Equally Being could refer to the inwardness of
the Christian life whereby we are alone with God, Intelligence
could refer to the intelligent personal relationship between the
Christian and God, and Bliss could refer to the communion of
the saints. Further Being could signify God in his unmanifest
aspect, Intelligence could signify God in his incarnate aspect,
and Bliss could signify God in his immanent aspect. Moreover, Being could be linked with a spirituality of transcendence, Intelligence with a spirituality of personalism, and Bliss
with a spirituality of immanence. There is a distant similarity
between some of this type of thinking and the work of some
of the early Fathers such as St. Augustine who had thought
of the Trinity in terms of the analogy of being, knowledge
and love. However, the difference is that Indian Christian
thought has placed more stress upon the experiential and
practical outworkings of the doctrine of the Trinity rather
than concentrating upon the doctrine for its own sake. In this
it has been aided by the traditional Indian perception that
truth must not be merely intellectually formulated but actually lived. Indeed the Sanskrit word *Sat* means both Being
and Truth. In order to follow God who is Absolute Truth we
must *live* the truth as well as express the truth in theological
terms.

(c) Sen and the Trinity. An early example of this kind of theology
lies in Keshab Chandra Sen, who lived from 1838 to 1884.
In his *Acknowledged Christ of the Hindu Renaissance* M M Thomas
has shown how a number of Indians responded to the Gospel
in significant ways without actually becoming Christians, and
prominent among them was Sen[7]. Indeed one of the most

remarkable developments in the whole history of Christian theology may well be the theological contribution made by these Indian thinkers who never technically became Christians. Sen went further in theological reflection on the Trinity than had Ram Mohan Roy who had been unitarian in his approach[8]. In a paper of 1882 Sen spoke of 'That Marvellous Mystery—the Trinity'[9]. He pointed out that the Trinity and *Saccidananda* were similar notions of who the Godhead is. The Father, he said, is the Creator, the still God, the 'I am' of the Godhead, who is Force, the True, and *Sat*. The Son, he said, is the Example, the journeying God, the 'I love' of the Godhead, who is Wisdom, the Good and *Cit*. The Holy Spirit, he said, is the Sanctifier, the returning God, the 'I save' of the Godhead, who is Holiness, the Beautiful, and *Ananda*. According to Sen, the Trinity can be seen to operate through the analogy of an equal triangle whose summit is the Father, one side represents the descent of the Son to earth, the base is Christ at work in the regeneration of mankind, and the other side represents the Holy Spirit taking regenerated mankind back up to the Father. Sen did not remain at the level of intellectual dogmas or theological models. He despised the West for doing just that. The Christ who had descended to earth, he pointed out, had made His abode in Asia, and any doctrine of the Trinity in terms of *Saccidananda* must lead on to living encounter with God in Christ or it would be worthless. Sen typifies the Indian stress upon theological truth as something that must be realised within and lived without. Truth is not merely abstract intellectual theories, it is following the example of the divine humanity of Christ in our outward lives, and it is 'being in God' as 'Christ is in the Father' in our inward lives, through the prompting of the Spirit.

(d) The Trinity and Brahman. Keshab Chandra Sen opened up a number of the themes that were to be developed by Indian Christians themselves. Before we examine this development in more detail let us pause in order to glance at the second adaptation of Indian thought made by Indian Christians. In addition to giving Christian content and form to the concept of *Saccidananda*, they also pressed into service the important

Indian idea that God as *Brahman* (Ultimate Reality) is both without qualities (*nirguna*) and with qualities (*saguna*). As *nirguna* he cannot be known in himself for he is beyond this phenomenal world and transcends what can be positively known; however, as *saguna* he does show himself to the world as having qualities and form in the shape of a personal God (*Ishvara*). In adapting this strand of Indian thought Indian Christians have had to avoid various traps, notably the *Advaita Vedanta* notion that Brahman is basically impersonal and that his personal *saguna* form is of secondary importance[10]. Given that these traps have been successfully bypassed, Indian Christians have begun to teach the wider church new insights into the meaning of the Trinity. As *nirguna Brahman*, God is greater than anything that can be conceived. He is not reduced to the level of anthropomorphism or even human analogies. He can never be pinned down; he can never be adequately conceptualised; He cannot be known in himself; there are areas of God's being beyond the personalism we see in Christ. And yet *Brahman* is also *saguna*. He is the personal *Ishvara* as well as the ultimate *Brahman*. He is the Creator as well as the One beyond creation. He is immanent as well as transcendent. He is accessible as well as remote. Indian Christians such as Brahmabandhab Upadhyaya[11], Panikkar, and others have shown how the first Person of the Trinity can be conceived of as Brahman, God without qualities, and the second Person of the Trinity can be seen as *Ishvara*, God with qualities. Christ makes the invisible God visible, and gives personhood to the unmanifest God. The working out of the meaning of the first two persons of the Trinity in terms of *nirguna* and *saguna Brahman* has been subtly done by Indian Christians in different ways. There is the material here for a new formulation of the doctrine in the thought-forms of India.

(e) (i) Trinitarian Spirituality. Now let us turn to the practical applications of the Trinity to the religious life on the part of Indian Christians. Notable in this venture has been Panikkar's *Trinity in World Religions* but others have contrib-uteb as well[12]. The main thrust of this work has been to relate the Trinity to the three religious ways outlined in the *Bhagavad Gita*, the ways (or *yogas*) of knowledge, devo-

tion, and works (*jnana, bhakti,* and *karma*). In the balanced Christian life these ways are related, not exclusive, in the same way that the persons of the Trinity are related and one. And yet they are not the same either, although used by one particular individual. According to Panikkar the spirituality depending on *karma* is related to God the Father, the spirituality depending on *bhakti* is related to God the Son, and the spirituality depending on *jnana* is related to God the Holy Spirit. For Panikkar these three types of spirituality are built into *all* religious traditions, as is a triune notion of God. It may be that this implied claim is inaccurate and that this theory works best in regard to Christianity and Indian thought. Nevertheless, and in a sense for this very reason, this idea can be helpful for Christian theology.

(ii) God the Father. God the Father is transcendent, beyond our sight, in light inacessible, wholly other, unknowable in himself. We can form mental images of God, but they point beyond themselves to One whom we cannot comprehend. We can only obey him, and stand in silence before the Absolute. We can offer him the service of our *karma* (ritual works) and we can adore him in silence through the images we make to represent him. We serve him and approach him with awe through the spirituality of *karma*. And so the spirituality associated with the first Person of the Trinity is that of *karma*, the service that we offer in obedience to God's holy otherness and the ritual adoration with which we respond to his majestic awe.

(iii) God the Son. God the Son is associated with the spirituality of *bhakti* which involves our personal love for God. Christ shows above all the personhood of God. He can be seen as a Person in a way that would not be true of God the Father or God the Holy Spirit. Panikkar points out that the early church notion that God is in three 'Persons' can restrict the fullness of God's being by limiting him to human analogies. Christ is the Personhood of God, He is the Lord, He is *Ishvara.* He is the link with God whom we know not so much in himself but through the Lord. He is the 'Thou' whereby we know the Absolute whom he

mediates. We know him through the spirituality of love, devotion, and prayerful relationship. According to Panikkar the Lord is present in all religious traditions whether known or unknown. He is fully shown through the medium of the church but he is present, though perhaps unknown, in other traditions. Others are therefore 'saved' by Christ who uses their tradition as normal channels to lead them to God. At this point Panikkar is universalising the western notion of Christ so that he can be visualised in non-western and non-Greek categories. And yet this Lord, this Logos, who cannot be confined to human boundaries is the Divine Person to whom we respond in love and prayer and devotion. He is the Lord of *bhakti* with whom we enjoy an I–Thou relationship.

(iv) God the Holy Spirit. God the Holy Spirit is associated with the spirituality of intuitive inwardness. He is immanent. He is not Other, he is not Person, he is not One with whom we enter into relationship—He is One whom we realise in the depths of our being. He is the Ground of our being beyond our outward self and we realise him inwardly through silence, through inwardness through union of our own deepest self with the Spirit of God. We are now in the realm of mysticism and inward realisation, not that of devotion or that of adoration of transcendent majesty. We are in the realm of the Spirit.

(v) Implications. I have summarised a lot of intricate ideas rather quickly in high-lighting this important concept of the 'three spiritualities of the Trinity'. This Indian Christian theological reflection is important for general theology in various subtle respects. It is also helpful in more direct ways. For part of the battle in the western world lies in the area of spirituality rather than in the realm of ideas. The western church has tended to stress the conceptual, the ethical, and the organisational aspects of religion rather than the experiential. The popular success of certain eastern movements almost surely lies in their stress upon the inward elements of religious life. The Christian church in its past history has not been lacking in deep spirituality but this feature is not conspicuously present at the moment.

It is likely that it may be revived by the stimulus given by Indian Christians and others who have been influenced by other religious groups who *have* given a central stress to inward spirituality[13]. Indeed the strength of the Indian Christian reflection on the Trinity is this. In addition to dwelling upon the difference in unity within the godhead, it has also stressed the difference in unity within Christian spirituality. It has made the point that ritual worship of God, loving devotion to God, and inward realisation of God are related aspects of an integral spirituality which finds concrete expression in service for God in the world. All of these different aspects of spirituality are bound up together. Just as God is transcendent, yet personal, yet immanent, so also we need to worship God in his transcendence, love him in his personhood, and realise him in his immanence. At the end of the day these are not three different spiritualities, they are different aspects of the same spirituality just as there is one triune God. This would appear to be an important contribution to Christian theology which, in its western garb, has tended to stress the role of Christ rather than that of the Trinity and the role of involvement rather than that of spirituality in the wider sense.

(f) Fakirbhai and the Trinity. A recent Indian Christian thinker Dhanjibhai Fakirbhai has added an important element to this debate about the spiritualities of the Trinity. He has given a deeper Indian structure to this type of theology by expressing it in poetic and dialogue form[14]. Whereas Panikkar utilised the theological method common in Indian philosophy, namely commentary on key verses of sacred texts, Fakirbhai uses the dialogue method found in the *Bhagavad Gita*. Both these methods are Indian and important for future theological developments on a world scale. The dogmatic tome may have become standard in western theological work; the same does not necessarily follow for theological work elsewhere. However, Fakirbhai is also significant for the added dimension he gives to the content of trinitarian spirituality. For him the centre of Christian theology lies in the conviction that God is Love. God is *Saccidananda* and the spiritualities of

karma, *bhakti* and *jnana* are relevant for the Christian. But overarching *Saccidananda* and these three spiritualities is Love. God is above all Love and to follow him is above all to love. 'So it is,' he says, 'that the complete *yoga* of Action, Worship and Knowledge (*karma, bhakti* and *jnana*) is attained through the Way of Love (*prema yoga*).' Fakirbhai adds to the discussion in two ways. In the first place, Panikkar tends to limit *karma* to ritual and sacrifice which is one of its Sanskrit meanings whereas Fakirbhai stresses the meaning of *karma* as service or action. A crucial element of involvement is added to Panikkar's view of spirituality. In the second place, Fakirbhai stresses the role of love as the key factor. In fact he is not going as far beyond Panikkar as appears to be the case because Panikkar had made *bhakti* and the Lord his key link and he had done this because loving devotion was central to the Trinity and to spirituality. Fakirbhai weakens the meaning of *bhakti* to 'worship' instead of 'loving devotion' and introduces the word *prema* to denote 'love' in a stronger sense than is implied in *bhakti*[15]. Nevertheless they are not far apart in asserting that the Personhood of Christ is central to the Trinity and that personal devotion is important in any authentic Christian spirituality. In the third place, and here I interpret the theological and existential quest of Indian Christian theology, Fakirbhai is indicating that in fact there are four kinds of spirituality arising out of trinitarian theology, namely those of worship, action, love, and knowledge. Fakirbhai makes love the controlling factor; other Indian Christians would make one of the other three predominant; and yet these four elements tend to appear in one form or another. In their understandable desire to enable their theology to arise out of the Christian doctrine of the Trinity and the three *yogas* of the *Bhagavad Gita*, Indian Christians have felt in duty bound to speak in terms of three spiritualities whereas in practice they have alluded to four. It is fascinating to reflect that the *Bhagavad Gita* also cites three ways of spirituality (knowledge, love and action) but also uses the word *karma* in two senses, namely those of action and ritual; to that extent the *Bhagavad Gita* is also alluding to four types of spirituality while mentioning only three in a formal sense.

(g) Practical outworkings. This whole development is tremendously important for wider Christian theology and life. Different churches at different times have emphasised one or perhaps more than one of these ways. Sometimes churches or individual Christians have stressed the primacy of worship, regular attendance at the public celebration of preaching and the sacraments. At other times they have stressed the centrality of loving God in Christ—he is the Friend whom we love as well as the Master whom we worship, and by commitment to him personally we enter into a devotional relationship with him. This relationship may be a quiet one as in the case of *bhakti* or it may be an emotional one as in the case of *prema*, the point is that it is a devotional relationship. At other times Christians have stressed the need for action, service, and involvement in the world. This has been the springboard for the expansion of Christian hospitals, schools, and welfare services. Especially in the case of America this sort of activism has been encouraged as being not only integral to but central to the Christian life. At other times, more rarely and mainly in the past, Christians have stressed the need for a strong inner life of meditation and contemplation and inwardness on the supposition that the Kingdom of God is within as well as without and that constant practice of the presence of God is crucial to the Christian life. Indian Christians are in the process of pointing out to us that all four ways are integral to the full Christian life. They do not exclude but include each other. They are not separate but related. They are all necessary. If any one of them is missing then the fullness of the Christian life is not there. This is a lesson that the Church may learn in our time to her great benefit in so many places and in so many ways. This intuition about the integral nature of the Christian life has been derived from a dual source, on the one hand Indian thought, especially the *Bhagavad Gita*, and on the other hand the doctrine of the Trinity. Indian Christian theologians are showing us that we are called upon as Christians to live in this way because God the Trinity mirrors this integral life in his own nature.

3. INDIAN RELIGION AND MALE AND FEMALE ASPECTS OF THE TRINITY

(a) Background

(i) New interest in God as Mother. In recent years Christian theologians have taken a new interest in the possibility of talking about God as Mother, in the feasibility of a female theology, and in the notion that the divine may be seen as feminine as well as masculine. Clearly feminine theology as a movement has been a spur to this renewal of interest in the female aspects of Godhead. One suspects that this renewal of interest is more than a passing phase. Not only is a deeper consciousness of the feminine emerging in cultures in different parts of the globe; influences as various as Jungian psychology and other world religions are making the point that male and female are complementary[16]. If this is true of human nature, is it untrue of the divine nature?

(ii) Male connotations of the Trinity. Part of the problem is that Christian theology has inherited a masculine view of God from its Hebrew background. God was seen as Father. Not only that, he was portrayed in male images such as Warrior and Ruler. Jesus Christ was born into the world as a man. It was natural to describe Jesus Christ, as the Apostles' Creed puts it, in terms of 'His only Son, our Lord'. Both Father and Son were portrayed in masculine terms. Attempts have been made to depict the Holy Spirit in terms of the feminine Sophia. However, the traditional Christian theology image of God the Trinity has been in masculine terms. If there were space we could qualify this statement but in general terms it rings true. The Christian view of God is basically male; the Trinity is conceptualised in the masculine. The relationships within the Trinity are conceived not in male–female but in male terms.

The main Christian theological attempt to introduce a feminine image into Christian thought has centred upon the Virgin Mary who was seen in some theological circles as the mother of God. Nevertheless, although the Virgin Mary might be seen as *theotokos*, she was not seen as God. Although venerated, she was not taken up into the divine.

If the mother of God was gloriously female, God the Trinity remained male.

(b) Christian Trinity and Hindu Thought

What light then can Christian theology gain on this important matter by engagement with Hindu thought?

(i) God as female in Hinduism. We see, in the first place, the importance the Hindu tradition has attached to God as female. This image of God as female has taken two main forms. One development was that male divinities had female consorts so that a male divinity such as Shiva would be partnered by a female divinity such as Parvati, or another male divinity Vishnu would be partnered by his consort Sri. A second development opened up the possibility for the female devinity to be worshipped in her own right. Indeed during medieval times Shakti, the goddess, became far more important than Brahma the creator god as a focus of devotion among Hindus. The three main personal divinities became Vishnu, Shiva and the Goddess. Trust, love and devotion were showered upon the Goddess in her various forms. She became an object of devotion in whom one placed one's faith and to whom one surrendered one's life. Midway between these two developments lies the extraordinary example of Radha. She emerges in the earlier Krishna traditions as one of the cowgirls, the *gopis*, who were enamored of Krishna. She later rises to a position of supreme importance among the cowgirls and becomes a consort of Krishna. She is worshipped jointly with Krishna. Later still, in some Krishna circles, she is given greater importance even than Krishna and is worshipped in her own right as a female God. As it is our purpose to illuminate Christian theology rather than describe the Hindu tradition we will refrain from piling up examples but it is clear that there is ample evidence within Hinduism of female consorts and goddesses[17].

However these examples cannot be transferred even by a convoluted hermeneutics into the Christian context. They show the importance within the Hindu tradition of a female image of divinity. To that extent they make the significant point that another great religious tradition has emphasised the feminine aspect of the Godhead. But they can hardly be moved directly from the Hindu to the Christian context.

(ii) Vedanta and Sankhya thought. Help is forthcoming albeit indirectly from another part of the Hindu tradition, namely its philosophy. We saw earlier in this chapter how Indian Christian theology enlarged its view of the Trinity through dialogue with Vedanta thought. Another of the six Hindu philosophical systems is Sankhya. On the face of it, Sankhya is very different from Vedanta. Yet both systems appear together in the Bhagavad Gita; and in the Vedanta-sara of the fifteenth century AD and the work of Vijnan-abhiksu in the sixteenth century they appear side by side[18]. They are seen as complementary truths.

Sankhya is a dualistic system based upon the interplay of two elements, Purusha and Prakriti. Purusha is passive and Prakriti is active. Purusha although passive works upon Prakriti in order to bring it into active play. Prakriti includes three different but intertwining strands called gunas. If Prakriti were left to itself, these three strands would remain in equilibrium. However set into motion by the influence of Purusha they are in constant interplay. Thus Purusha and Prakriti are complementary. The one is passive and the other is active. Yet lying behind the inter-related triune strands of Prakriti rests the motivating passivity of Purusha[19].

(c) Male and female aspects of the Trinity. Of itself, Sankhya has little or no connection with God the Trinity except in the formal sense that Prakriti contains three inter-related strands and that it is complemented by Purusha. However when we link the Sankhya image to the rich notion of the Trinity achieved by the dialogue with Vedanta, and when we link this Sankhya/Vedanta imagery to notions already present in Christian mystical theology, I believe we gain potentially creative insights into God the Trinity. Alongside the masculine inter-relatedness of the persons of the Trinity there lies a complementary feminine aspect. If God the Father can be seen as a dynamic fountain who generates the Son and spirates the Spirit in an archetype of male procession within

the divine, lying behind there can be seen a motivating passivity. The Godhead is not necessarily seen in perfect completeness within the male trinitarian archetype. Alongside the fountain that is God is the abyss whence that fountain flows. Alongside the Logos that is the Word is the silence wherein it is uttered. Alongside the Light that is the Spirit is the darkness whence it radiates. Alongside the Trinity there is the abyss, the silence and the darkness that constitute the primal feminine ground within the Godhead.

According to this theological scheme it is not necessary to question the maleness of the Christian Trinity. It constitutes a male archetype. But alongside it there is the motivating passivity that reflects a female ground within the Godhead. As Eckhart puts it in his mystical theology:

> The Trinity is only the manifestation of the Godhead. In the pure Godhead there is absolutely no activity. The soul attains to perfect beatitude only in throwing itself into the desert of the Godhead there where there are neither operations nor forms, to bury itself there and lose itself there in that wilderness where its ego is annihilated[20].

This desert, this abyss, this silence, this darkness that image the female ground of the Trinity are complementary to the male Trinity. The male Trinity remains intact but it is complemented by a female pole or ground within the wholeness of the Divine.

Others must develop further the implications of this theological insight[21]. By comparison with the Indian Christian theological work on the Trinity we glanced at earlier, it is abstruse. Nevertheless, it has obvious and important implications. It sounds echoes already recorded within Christian theology, but those echoes are triggered by dialogue with the Hindu tradition.

FOOTNOTES

1. A good summary of modern Hindu thought is to be found in D S Sarma, *Hinduism Through the Ages* Bombay, 1973. M M Thomas, *The*

Acknowledged Christ of the Indian Renaissance, SCM, London, 1969, details the Christian influence upon the Hindu reformers.

2. Robin Boyd, *An Introduction to Indian Christian Theology* CLS, Madras, 1975, intimates this, as do the various publications of the Christian Institute for the Study of Religion and Society, Bangalore.

3. K Mathothu, *The Development of the Concept of Trimurti in Hinduism*, Palai, Kerala, 1974.

4. There are a number of reasons for this claim. Two important reasons are that the Goddess Shakti came to replace Brahma the Creator as an effective focus of later Hindu devotion; also that the three personal deities were seen as separate manifestations rather than as strictly trinitarian.

5. *Saccidananda* is the union in Sanskrit of the three words *sat, cit,* and *ananda*.

6. It is interesting to note that the Arabic language too has not so radically divorced the meaning of the words Being and Truth.

7. Sen was a leader of the Brahmo Samaj; he had a deep attraction to Christ; he was also influenced in later life by the Hindu mystic Ramakrishna.

8. Ram Mohan Roy engaged in dialogue with Marshman, one of the Serampore missionaries, and he converted another, Adam, to unitarian Christianity.

9. Keshab Chandra Sen, *Keshab Chandra Sen's Lectures in India*, Cassell, London, 1909.

10. As formulated by the followers of the great Indian philosopher Shankara, *Advaita* posits two levels of truth, the empirical and the higher levels. A leap of realisation is required to pass from one to the other, and they are discontinuous.

11. Brahmabandhab Upadhyaya (1861–1907), a Bengali Brahmin, was baptised in 1891.

12. R Panikkar, *The Trinity and World Religions* CLS, Madras, 1970.

13. The rise of the notions of Christian Yoga and Christian Zen is evidence of this.

14. D Fakirbhai, *Kristopanishad* (CISRS, 1965); and *The Philosophy of Love* (ISPCK, Delhi, 1966).

15. The *bhakti* of the earlier devotional movements influenced by Ramanuja was moderate and restrained; some of the later devotional movements were more ecstatic in nature and *prema* indicates a more emotional content in the devotional attitude.

16. See John A Sanford, *Invisible Partners*, Paulist, New York, 1980. See also Erich Neumann's classic, *The Great Mother: An Analysis of the Archetype*, Princeton University Press, Princeton, 1955.

17. See M Brown, *God as Mother*, Claude Stark, Cape Cod, 1974; W C Beane, *Myth, Cult and Symbols in Sakti Hinduism: A Study of the Indian Mother Goddess*, E J Brill, Leiden, 1977; David R Kinsley, *The Sword and the Flute: Kali and Krishna*, University of California Press, Berkeley and Los Angeles, 1975.

18. Heinrich Zimmer, *Philosophies of India*, Princeton University Press, Princeton (Bollingen Paperback 1971 Second Printing) p 314.

19. Sankhya evolved radically over a long period of time. For a more static account see Zimmer, *ibid*, pp 314–332.

20. See E Colledge and B McGinn (eds), *Meister Eckhart: The Essential Sermons, Commentaries, Treatises, and Defense*, Paulist Press, New York, 1981, p 198.

21. I am indebted to my colleague and friend, Professor Ewert Cousins of Fordham University, for conversation on this topic. I trust that he or possibly Jungian scholars may develop its implications further.

CHAPTER EIGHT

CONCLUSION

In the introduction we stated that, like a piece of music, this book is centred upon a main theme, *Christian Theology and World Religions: A Global Approach*. Throughout the course of this book we have played upon nine variations of this main theme. We have given a comprehensive treatment of all the topics implied in this title. In dealing with these topics, in playing these variations, we have interpreted and expanded upon the dominant harmony that is our master theme. We dare to claim that we have done this in a more complete way than has been attempted before.

The time has come, in our conclusion, to return more directly to our title and to regroup our material in a way that will sum up more succinctly what we have been saying.

Let us switch the analogy, for a moment, from music to light. In this work, we have broken up our topic into smaller constituent parts, and we have dealt with each of them in turn. It has been rather like putting a beam of light through a prism. When this happens, the beam of light is split up into its constituent colours of red, blue, yellow, purple, orange, etc, so that the one beam of light is transformed into the colours of a rainbow. The colours of the rainbow are attractive in themselves, but ultimately they are part of a greater whole. It is the same with this book. Our aim is to return to the original beam of light, the dominant theme, and to summarise the whole.

This is not so easy to accomplish as would appear to be the case at first sight. For contained within the title of the book, and within the dominant theme, are three sections, three movements: *Christian Theology*, *World Religions*, and *A Global Approach*. In this final chapter, we will look at each of these in turn. In so doing, we will seek to gather together the total discussion of this book, and to recapitulate our nine variations in a more integral way; we will seek the whole rainbow that transcends the different colours that are parts of it. We will begin with *World Religions*, continue with *Christian Theology*, and go on to *A Global Approach*; we will end by looking at the inter-relationships between the three.

I. WORLD RELIGIONS

Throughout this book, we have stressed the need for Christian theology to have a much deeper understanding of world religions, both for their own sake, and for the light they can shed on Christian theology. The ignorance of many Christian theologians concerning world religions is unhelpful. While understandable in the past, it is no longer fully excusable. World religions can no longer be ignored in a global world; if they are, it is at the peril of Christian theology.

(a) Their vastness. We have seen how a major problem for the Christian theologian is the sheer vastness and complexity of other religions. Let it be admitted that it is also a problem for the religious studies scholar who can concentrate more upon world religions without having the same need to be proficient in Christian theology. It is folly to suppose that anyone, let alone the Christian theologian, can obtain a good knowledge of all the world's religious traditions. Quite apart from the range of knowledge needed to master any one religious tradition, there is the great variety of religions that have been and are present on the face of the globe. To remind ourselves of the depth of the problem, let us look briefly at six different varieties of world religions.

(i) In the first place, there are the living major religious traditions of the world. Five of them can reasonably be classed as major: the Buddhist, Christian, Hindu, Jewish, and Muslim traditions. They have an impressive history, a worldwide presence, and a complex structure which compound the problems involved in trying to understand them.

(ii) Other religious traditions are living, they are present

and active in the world today, but it is a moot point as to whether they can be classed as major: for example the Parsis, the Sikhs, the Jains, the Confucians, the Taoists, the Shintoists, and the Baha'is. Although not major in the normally accepted sense of the word, they are unique and significant in their own right.

(iii) A third factor on the present-day religious scene is the presence of a number of what might be called alternative religions: sects and cults of one sort or another. I refer to groups such as the Jehovah's Witnesses, Seventh Day Adventists, Mormons, Spiritualists, Swedenborgians, Unification Church, the so-called New Religions of Japan, the cargo cults of Melanesia, the Rastafarians, and so forth. Whether they should be designated as world religions is problematic. Nevertheless it is estimated that in the United States alone there are something over 900 Christian sects, and 600 alternative religious traditions with no roots in Christianity.

(iv) A fourth segment can be summed up under the heading of primal religion: the religious life of primal tribes scattered across the face of the earth. There are in fact thousands of these tribes each with their own religious life. There are therefore thousands of primal religions. They lack writing; therefore they lack scriptures and historical documents. The hallmarks of their religious life tend to be myths and rituals and symbols that are handed down from generation to generation.

(v) In the fifth place there are religious traditions that are dead. Human beings at one time had access to transcendence through these archaic religions but they are with us no more. We rest content with mentioning Palaeolithic and Neolithic religion, Mesopotamian and Egyptian religion, Greek and Roman religion, Gnostic and Manichaean religion, and the Aztecs, Incas and Mayas of the Americas.

(vi) A final possible set of what Tillich termed 'quasi-religions' comprises secular alternatives to religion such as Marxism and Humanism. It is doubtful whether they can

be called religions in any full sense. Nevertheless the term 'quasi-religions' has a meaningful resonance.

Such is the vastness and complexity of the field of 'world religions'! It would be ludicrous for Christian theologians to attempt to become knowledgeable in them all. Selectivity is necessary. In this book, we have concentrated upon the major living religions, and to a smaller extent upon African primal religion, Chinese religion, and Marxism. I think many Christian theologians will see the need to concentrate mainly upon the major living religions. Religious Studies scholars can concentrate, if they wish, upon the sects and cults, the primal religions, the dead archaic religions, the non-major living religions, and Marxism and Humanism as quasi-religions. In a global world, it is the global religions that are of main interest to the Christian theologian.

(b) A model for understanding world religions. How then can any particular world religion be understood? Contained within this book is a model for understanding any world religion. This model presents a grid or framework within which any religious tradition can be understood. Lying behind the model is the notion that religious traditions are not the same. However neither are they so different that there is no basis for comparison or mutual understanding.

The model suggests that every religious tradition has lying behind it a notion (indeed a reality) of transcendence. How is this transcendent reality made available to human beings on earth? The model suggests that in each religious tradition there is a mediating focus whereby ultimate reality, which would otherwise be ineffable, is made available to persons in the living of life.

At the more observable level, the model points to eight elements that are present in all religious traditions. They are not present with the same weight in each religion because religions are different and they stress different elements in a different way. Nevertheless they are present in some way or another in every religious tradition. All traditions contain a religious community; a ritual element including worship, sacraments and festivals; an ethical element which brings out the need for living a good life; recommendations for social and political involvement in wider society; scriptural texts which contain basic myths; and emphases on certain doctrines. Every tradition uses the aesthetic elements of music, painting, sculpture, architecture, and general litera-ture, and all of them emphasise the element of spirituality. Christianity stresses doctrine more than other traditions, Buddhism stresses the spirituality of meditation more than others. Jews and Muslims stress the importance of moral and ethical injunctions more than others, and Hindus stress social involvement through caste more than others.

Underlying this framework and the transcendent reality and mediating focus to which these eight elements point, lies the personal 'faith' of individuals themselves. Ultimately religious traditions have to do with persons. The eight elements, although important, are means to an end. The end is that a person should have meaningful contact with transcendent reality through a mediating focus. Religious traditions, through the way that they structure their eight elements, make this possible. By means of their religious community, rituals, ethics, social and political involvement, scriptures, concepts, aesthetics and spirituality, individuals can have access to transcendent reality through the mediating focus which works through these eight elements.

Our claim is that any religious tradition can be put into some sort of focus by means of this model. It applies less well to primal religions. It is questionable whether the quasi-religions have a strong view of transcendence or of spirituality. Nevertheless our feeling is that it is a good step forward towards a more congenial understanding of world religions—including Christianity!

(c) A global history of religion. In the past, Christian theologians and others became used to thinking in terms of the separate histories of separate religions. Thus one could look at the distinct histories of Islam, of the Hindu and the Buddhist traditions, of the Jews, and of the Christian tradition, and treat them as separate entities. This was accentuated by the tendency of Christian theologians to emphasise salvation history as being located within the history of the

Judaeo–Christian tradition, and after the Old Testament period it ceased to be obvious within the Jewish tradition! Another important reason for thinking in terms of separate histories of religion was the lack of a global vision that could encompass the whole of religious history.

For the first time in human history we are now able to see the past history of the globe as one. By the same token we are also now able to see the past history of religion in a global sense. What seemed to be the separate histories of separate religions can be seen to be part of a wider story. That story is the global history of religion. During the course of the book we have given a brief survey of this global history of religion. Thus Christianity can be seen within the same continuum of religious history as the other world religions. There is the rise of a new corporate self-consciousness that enables world religions to see their inter-connectedness as well as their separateness.

Therefore in addition to giving a model for understanding world religions, we have also shown how the separate histories of the world religions can be comprehended in a wider whole.

(d) Passing-over into world religions. So far the steps we have recommended for understanding world religions have been somewhat intellectual, albeit far-reaching. Our final stratagem for getting inside other religions has a more empathetic, even emotional, basis.

Our first steps, aimed at understanding the data of other religions, can be likened to the process known to phenomenologists as *epochè* (putting one's own views into brackets in order to understand the position of another). This tends to have a neutral even a slightly negative connotation. This is not the case with passing-over. This may be likened to the process known to the phenomenologists as *Einfühlung* (deep empathy). This involves active entering in to the thought-world and feeling-universe of another. It means seeing the universe, in some sense, through the eyes of our partner from another religion. It means exploring in our own consciousness their sense of being a Hindu, or being a Muslim. It means getting underneath the skin of our brother and sister, and seeing 'what makes them tick'. It involves some sort of active self-giving of ourselves in love and understanding so that the other person and their religion become 'real' to us.

At this point, understanding world religions means not only having a mental grasp of what the other person's religious community, rituals, ethics, social and political involvement, scripture, concepts, aesthetics, and spirituality are all about, and how it might be possible for that person through those elements to be in contact with transcendent reality. It means passing-over into the world-view of another person in such a way that we have a joyful sense of what their world-view means to them emotionally, in addition to what it means to us intellectually. It gives us access, in some small but poignant way, to their faith and their experience. We are no longer on the outside, we are—in however minute a way—on the inside.

(e) World religions and Religious Studies. The main avenue for gaining the above-mentioned understanding of world religions is through the medium of Religious Studies. The Christian theologian is dependent upon the work of Religious Studies for understanding of and insight into world religions. Religious Studies has a more direct concern in the study of world religions, it has more intimate access to the languages of the religious traditions concerned, and through the phenomeno-logical method it is engaged in understanding and inter-preting the religion of others.

However, the exercise of passing-over is a matter of heart as well as mind. It may well be, in some cases, that the Christian theologian has less knowledge than the Religious Studies scholar. But, because of a deep intention to penetrate the thought-world of another, the motivation to understand and love may take him or her further.

Usually the Christian theologian will take advantage of the work of others in the field of Religious Studies. Sometimes, and this is becoming less unlikely as the years go by, he or she will have a foot in both camps, like Gerhardus van der Leeuw. The Christian theologian will gain expertise in Religious Studies and will pass backwards and forwards between the two enterprises as the situation demands.

2. CHRISTIAN THEOLOGY

Our last comment takes us appropriately into our second section, that of Christian theology. In this book, we have spent much time in discussing Christian theology. We make no excuse for this fact, because this book is located in a series dealing with Christian theology and it is therefore right that we should have spent more space in dealing with Christian theology than in dealing with world religions.

We have not attempted to hide the fact that Christian theology is complex and plural. There is no monolithic Christian theology. There is no one way for Christian theology to approach other religions. We live in an age of plural theology and of plural Christianity. We must wait until the twenty-first century for another systematic theology in the mould of Barth or Tillich. In the meantime we live in an age of theological adventure and excitement but not theological agreement. We live at a time of Christian plurality and diversity within a wider framework of conviction that the Christian tradition, at any rate in intention, should be seen as a whole.

Let us rehearse our comments on Christian theology before going on to ally them with our work on world religions.

(a) Three kinds of theology. In a detailed chapter on the history of the development of the word 'theology', we made the point that theology has been defined in three ways.

In Graeco-Roman times theology was viewed as part of philosophy, and philosophy in turn was viewed as being part of a general education. In other words it was not necessary to belong to a particular religious tradition in order to be involved in theology. Theologia was an account of the gods of the Greek and Roman pantheons, and it was also an account of God. For example Aristotle's theological philosophy included his notion of the divine nature and of God as the unmoved Mover. A knowledge of the gods and of God was part of the general knowledge that was necessary to life in the Graeco-Roman world. It was not the theology of a particular religious community.

During the Christian era, theology became located within a particular religious ethos, namely that of the Christian

church. Theology was no longer just part of a general education; it was no longer merely an element within the humanities. Theology became the theology of a particular community.
It was the account of God and of those people who called
themselves Christians. This is the meaning of Christian
theology that we have used most consistently in these pages.

In recent times another meaning of theology has arrived in
the intellectual arena. After it was realised that there were
other world religions that had their own theologies, it seemed
to thinkers such as Wilfred Cantwell Smith that it was not
good enough to acquiesce in this situation of competing theologies. There was an overarching global theology, it seemed
to him, of which Christian, Muslim, Hindu and Jewish and
other theologies were parts. As far as he was concerned,
Christian theology viewed solely as the theology of the Christian community was too particular. Global theology must be
Christian but it must also be more than Christian. It must
be Muslim, Buddhist, Hindu, and Jewish at the same time.
The proper task for theology was to seek for universal theological categories that overshot the boundaries of particular
religious traditions and were true of all religions in our global
world.

While recognising that the other two views concerning
theology were present, we have concentrated upon the second
notion of Christian theology, namely it is the theology arising
out of the Christian community.

(b) Christian theology within Christianity as a world religion.
Granted that this is our view of Christian theology, we have
seen how it takes on a different hue when seen in the light of
Christianity as a world religion. What does it mean to say
that Christianity is a world religion?

(i) It means, firstly, that the Christian tradition must be
seen as a whole. Certainly it does contain different branches: Roman Catholic, Orthodox, Protestant of various
sorts, and so on. But it can no longer be defined in sectarian
terms. Christian theology is the theology, in principle, of
the whole Christian tradition. It cannot be limited, for
whatever reason, to the theology of part of the Christian

tradition. It is the whole theology of the whole church in the whole world.

(ii) It means, secondly, that Christianity is a world religion in a geographical sense. It is no longer confined to the western world. The mission of the church has gone into every corner of the world. Stephen Neill in his history of missions claims that only Nepal, Afghanistan, and Tibet are bereft of Christian mission. This is no longer true of Nepal, and it may well be untrue of Tibet and Afghanistan as well. The Christian community may be on a plateau in terms of numbers and influence in the West; it is expanding rapidly in Africa and Latin America, it is growing quickly in places like Korea and China. It is therefore no longer a western religion, but a world religion. The next Pope could conceivably be from the Third World. If the World Council of Churches were to move its headquarters from Geneva, it would conceivably go to a Third World city such as Nairobi.

(iii) It means, thirdly, that Christianity fits into the model of a world religion that we have used in this book. This has certain consequences for Christian theology. As we saw in our study of the development of the word 'theology', Christian theology has been applied mainly to doctrine, to concepts. Now the conceptual element is only one element among eight in our model of a religion. We therefore have the anomalous situation whereby Christian theology can refer, in a general sense, to the whole model of Christianity, and include all the eight elements that are part of the model. However in a particular, and perhaps more accurate sense it refers to only one of the eight elements in the model. What is Christian theology? Is it reflection upon Christianity as a whole, or is it reflection upon only the doctrinal aspect of the Christian tradition? This remains an unresolved question in wider Christian theology. In this book we have preferred to use it primarily in regard to the doctrinal element (and to a lesser extent the spirituality element) within the Christian tradition.

(c) The Complexity of Doctrinal Christian Theology. However, even if we restrict Christian theology to the doctrinal sphere it still remains a complex phenomenon. Even if we restrict it to the doctrinal sphere within western Christianity, it covers many areas. It may involve the aftermath of Bultmann's demythologising, neo-orthodoxies redolent of Barth, exploration into religious language, process theology, liberation theology, feminine theology, black theology, apologetics, creative evolution, theology of ministry, theology of mystical spirituality, new liturgics, reinterpretations of the Creed, new biblical theology, re-examination of the proofs for the existence of God, and so on. The ingenuity of doctrinal theological imagination is endless in the contemporary scene, and much of it is speaking to real problems in the western world. As we said earlier, a contemporary systematic theology is not in sight, and this position bespeaks energy and a plural dynamism in Christianity today.

(d) Non-western contribution to Christian theology. However, the situation is even more complex than the one painted above. For as we have demonstrated already, Christian theology is now global in the sense that it cannot be confined to what is happening in the western church. Not only growth but new ideas are emerging in indigenous Christian churches outside the western world. In this book, we have examined some of these new theological contributions made by the younger churches to global Christian theology.

The contributions that are being made are many and varied, coming as they do from different parts of the world, and from dialogue with different religions in different cultures.

It is the conviction of this author and an increasing number of Christian theologians in other parts of the western world (not to mention the eastern world) that the creative and original ideas are emanating from outside the West. Logic suggests that this must be the case. For in spite of the fertility of concepts within western theology, they inevitably arise within a milieu that is familiar. They originate within a realm of discourse that is already known, and therefore they can only constitute a rippling of waters that are set in place. The ideas thrown up by the dialogue of the younger churches with other religions, and by the grappling of Christian theology with the questions raised by non-western universes of thought, are inevitably more challenging and promising for real theological advance.

The systematic theology that will emerge in the twenty-first century will be deeply influenced by these ideas. Just as the theology of the early church was imbued with Greek thought, even though the first Christians were Christian Jews, so also the Christian theology of the twenty-first century will be imbued with insights from other cultures even though the modern church has been primarily a western church. The situation is changing before our eyes, and we have merely pointed to the tip of the iceberg as far as non-western Christian theology is concerned.

(e) Passing-over and returning. We wrote earlier about passing-over into other religions in order to understand them. As far as Christian theology is concerned (as opposed to Religious Studies) the point is both to pass-over and to return. Only in this way can the fruits of contacts with other religions and cultures be made available to Christian theology.

It is easier for Christians in non-western lands to achieve this 'dialogue on the march'. They are in contact with persons of other religious traditions in their everyday life. However, western Christians are increasingly in contact with people of other religions. The church is a world church. Whether Christians are in daily physical contact with persons of other traditions or not, there is an increasing challenge and imperative to pass-over into the world-views of other religions and to return recreated in vision. After all, Aquinas and his fellow Dominicans were not in physical contact with Aristotle and the early Greeks but this did not prevent them from passing-over into the world-view of Aristotle and returning to renew the theology of their day.

The world-view of medieval Europe was limited to contact with a rediscovered Aristotle. We are more lucky. The world is our theological parish. The great religions of the world are open to each other as has never been the case before in our present global environment. Within the confines of this book we have outlined some of the theological gains already made by contact with African religion and Chinese religion, and in relation to one particular doctrine, that of the Trinity. The actual gains are far wider than we have had the space to explore. We are on the threshold of some of the most momentous theological developments within the history of the Christian tradition.

3. OUR PRESENT GLOBAL SITUATION

Part of the title of this book reads *A Global Approach*. We have paid less attention to those words than they perhaps merit. Yet they are momentous. For the fact that we now live in a global world is central to our concerns.

We have already seen the importance of global factors in three ways. We saw firstly that the major living religions of the world are the key partners in dialogue for Christian theology insofar as they are crucial for the global situation, whereas other non-major living religions, sects and cults, primal religions, and archaic dead religions are not. We saw secondly that it is now possible to think in terms of a global history of religion that embraces all the religious traditions of the world. From our vantage-point in the global present, we can look back upon the past history of religion and see in what appear to be separate histories of separate religions a global pattern that is apparent now, but was not so in the past. We saw thirdly that Christianity itself is a global religion, and that Christian theology is now a global theology. The Christian tradition is no longer embalmed in the western part of the planet, it has a global presence. Christian theology is no longer hidebound by the categories of western thought, it incorporates insights from the rest of the globe.

Overshadowing even these considerations is the global situation itself in its entirety. It is becoming clear that if the human race is unable to adjust its thinking to global proportions it may well perish. By the same token it is also becoming clear that the global resources available to the world are far richer than was formerly imagined. If our thinking can be adjusted to global proportions, our global prospects are brighter than ever before. Since the exploding of the atom bombs at Hiroshima and Nagasaki, since the American astronauts saw the earth from the perspective of the moon, our horizons have become global. We share the threat of nuclear holocaust opened up in the long term by the first atomic explosions; we share the promise of global co-operation envisaged from the moon when the earth was really seen to be one. We have indicated in our analysis that any long-term thinking about Christian theology and world religions must be done against the backdrop of our global situation: we must take a global approach.

Global problems have been more obvious, at first sight, than global opportunities. The ecological threat to our global existence is obvious: the dying out of various species, the diminishing of the rain forests and woodlands, the pollution of our environment, the using up of non-renewable natural resources of minerals and energy, the contamination of the atmosphere and biosphere, the threat to the ozone shield, the cumulative effect of nuclear experiments. Human misunderstanding of other humans is also obvious at a global level: the poverty gap between rich and poor nations, the political differences between East and West, the economic differences between North and South, the mounting spiral of world population, the refugee problem, the sexual revolution, racial discrimination, terrorism, unemployment, and increasing nuclear proliferation and tension. Moral and spiritual matters also have a global dimension: what are we to do with the space that surrounds our globe and the sea that covers our globe, what is the meaning for our globe of the new discoveries in genetics and electronics, how is the perennial search for meaning affected by our global situation, are we affected by a global spiritual malaise? Our global problems are only too obvious.

Obvious too are our global opportunities. The natural, human, and spiritual riches of all cultures, religions and civilisations are open to all the people on earth in a way that has never been true before.

The global situation offers an unprecedented challenge and stimulus to Christian theology and world religions to forsake their parochial concerns and to seek the wellbeing of the planet as a whole over and above the vested interests of particular parties, or even of nation states.

4. CHRISTIAN THEOLOGY AND WORLD
RELIGIONS: A GLOBAL APPROACH

What then is or should be the relations between Christian theology and world religions in a global world?

(a) Christian theological attitudes to other religions. We summarised, in one of our chapters, the seven possible theological attitudes that Christian theology can take towards other religions. This has been the classical stance taken by Christian theology in relation to other religions: to define what attitudes can be adopted towards other religions. It remains relevant. We saw that Christians down the ages, and Christians today, have adopted and can adopt any one of seven possible theological attitudes to other religions ranging from exclusivism through discontinuity theology and dialogue theology to relativism. Circumstances may alter theological cases. For example, the attitude taken by Christians towards Hindus may be different in Nepal where there are very few Christians, from South India where there are millions of Christians; the attitude towards Muslims may be different in Arabia where there are very few Christians, from Nigeria where there are many Christians. The question what theological attitude should Christians take towards other religions remains a necessary theological enquiry at local levels and at a world level.

(b) Renewal of Christian theology by contact with other religions. More important, in a global perspective, is the question of how Christian theology can renew itself through contact with other religions. In this book we have experimented with the technique of passing-over into other religions and returning from that experience with rich insights for the renewal of Christian theology. We saw how African religion has much to teach Christian theology about the communion of saints, about the relations between God, humanity and nature, about the importance of symbols, dreams and visions, about religious healing, about the significance of initiation and death, about the church as a community, and about the meaning of the good life. We saw how the Chinese Christian dialogue with Chinese Religion and Chinese Marxism has

much to teach Christian theology about being in the world
yet not being of the world, about transcendence, about prayer
and spirituality, about Christian and inter-faith ecumenism,
and about the relations between transcendence, humanity
and nature. We saw how Indian religion has much to teach
Christian theology about the central Christian doctrine of the
Trinity.

If Christian theology is to speak to the global situation it
is essential that it should globalise itself by meaningful contact
with the other world religions. This is beginning to happen.
There has only been space to intimate a small proportion of
the creative theological renewal movements stimulated by the
contacts between Christian theology and world religions. The
trickle is developing into a swelling stream, and this must
happen if Christian theology is to become truly global in
outlook. The days of the western captivity of Christian
theology are at an end. The period of tutelage is over; the era
of partnership has arrived. A global church is facing the
challenge of producing a global theology to speak to a global
world.

(c) Dialogue with other religions for the creating of a global future.
However, Christian theology can go only so far in renewing
itself by contact with other religions in order to speak to the
global situation. For Christians, transcendent reality is God
the Trinity; for Christians the mediating focus is Jesus Christ.
Themes, truths, insights can be incorporated into Christian
theology by passing-over into and returning from other
religions: they are incorporated into an ongoing Christian
theology that is ever-changing and ever-new because it is
centred upon the ineffable symbol of God the Trinity and the
mediating focus of Jesus the Christ.

Other religious traditions are undergoing the same process.
For example, the Buddhist tradition in South East Asia is
looking to Christian models of social and political involvement
partly to reverse a past other-worldly attitude which has
become threatened by Marxist concerns for this world that
have led to Marxism's spread in South East Asia. It is impossible to understand the modern Hindu renaissance as seen in
the work of men such as Ram Mohan Roy, Keshub Chandra

Sen, the Tagores, Ramakrishna, Vivekananda, Aurobindo, Radhakrishnan, and Gandhi without taking seriously the Hindu passing-over into Christianity and returning with some of its riches.

Religious traditions are therefore undergoing constant change but they do not become carbon copies of each other. They remain distinct. Because this is so, the process of dialogue between religions is very important. The Christian dialogue with other religions is not only aimed at renewing Christian theology although this is the case. It is also aimed at creating a global future wherein religions can borrow from one another yet disagree with each other, can gain converts from each other yet respect one another, can live creatively together in a diversity that is transcended by a vision of global harmony that they all seek.

The dialogue with other religions is important therefore not only for what Christian theology can get out of it but also for what other religions and the human family in general can get out of it. We have spent relatively little time in these pages on this specific theme yet it has been implicit in much of what we have written.

(d) Global theology of religion and perennial philosophy. We have given quite a lot of space to the work on global theology of Wilfred Cantwell Smith, and to the work on perennial philosophy of Huston Smith and Seyyed Hossein Nasr. We saw that Cantwell Smith's concern is to begin with a vision of global theology that contains universal theological categories that are germane to all religions and to work back from that to Christian theology (and Muslim theology and Jewish theology and other particular theologies). According to this viewpoint Christian theology is one species of theology along with many others within global theology. The conceptual and moral force of theology in a global world should be centred at the global level rather than at the parochial level of Christian theology and other particular theologies.

As far as *philosophia perennis* is concerned we saw that this school of thought also begins with a universal view of what religious reality essentially is, and it works back from this core of global spirituality that it claims is common to all true

religion to the outward religious traditions that inhabit our
globe. Therefore the perennial philosophy also places Christian theology into a wider whole. It sees it to be secondary
rather than primary. Insofar as Christian theology is centred
at the level of the mind, or even if it is centred at the level of
the heart or soul, it does not wrestle with the true inwardness
of human beings which has to do with their spirit. There is
a perennial philosophy, an inward spirituality, at the heart of
all religions. This is the key to them rather than the outward
doctrines with which they clothe their experiences.

We saw the attraction of these two viewpoints because of
their obvious relevance to the global situation. The search for
a global theology and the search for a global spirituality are
attractive propositions in the search for a viable global future
for humanity.

The question that we have raised, quite apart from any
particular criticisms that can be made of these viewpoints, is
whether they are the proper province of Christian theology?

The thought of Wilfred Cantwell Smith and of *philosophia
perennis* lie at the inter-sections of religious studies and
theology. However our conclusion was that their resting-
ground does not lie within Christian theology as we have
portrayed it. We have stated that Christian theology is
primarily the theology arising out of the Christian tradition,
it is the theology of Christians and to that extent it does
have a particular connotation. Christian theology, as it has
developed down the ages, does not accept without question
that it is merely one species within a wider genus called
theology. It does not accept, without question, that there is
a transcendent unity of all religions based upon a perennial
philosophy common to all traditions. Indeed such enquiries
are not its proper province. They belong to a different enterprise that may appropriately be termed theology of religion
which in turn belongs more properly to the human enquiry
that comes under the heading of religious studies.

(e) Christian theology and religious studies. Running through our
whole discussion has been a debate about the relationship
between Christian theology and religious studies. Our
conclusion is that they are different but complementary. They

also are influenced by each other. Christian theology needs
religious studies as a source of information about world
religions, religious studies needs the stimulus of Christian
theology to enable it to take more seriously the transcendent
element within religion in general.

We saw in our discussion how Christian theology has a
more particular stress upon a specific religious tradition,
namely Christianity whereas religious studies has a theoreti-
cally equal concern for all the world's religions. We saw how
Christian theology inevitably has a vested interest in theology
as such, whereas religious studies uses other disciplines such
as phenomenology, history, sociology, psychology, anthropology, philosophy, and so on. We saw how Christian
theology has a primary concern for the conceptual element
(and to a lesser extent the spirituality element) in religion
whereas religious studies has an equal interest in the elements
of religious community, ritual, ethics, social and political
involvement, scripture, aesthetics, concepts, and spirituality.
We saw how Christian theology has a stress upon God (*theologia* is an account of God) as seen from the Christian perspective of God as mediated by Christ whereas religious studies
is content to view impartially concepts of transcendence that
are found in all religions without feeling the need to
pronounce that one of them is normative. Theology of religion
becomes a viable possibility for religious studies, albeit a
difficult one, whereas for Christian theology it is much more
problematical.

Christian theology and religious studies, in our view, are
therefore different but complementary. Without religious
studies, Christian theology and other particular theologies
tend to be parochial when they should be global in intent.
Without Christian theology and other particular theologies,
religious studies tends to be abstract.

However Christian theology has an obvious need of
religious studies in our emerging global situation. In order to
work out attitudes and relationships to other religions, it
needs knowledge about other religions that can be provided
by religious studies. In order to pass-over meaningfully into
other religions and to return in order to renew itself, Christian
theology needs the deep insights about other religions that

are available in religious studies. In order to engage in dialogue with other traditions for the creating of a global future, Christian theology needs the informed help of religious studies. In order to take the global situation seriously and to resist gravitational pull back into parochial interests and global irrelevance, Christian theology needs the promptings of religious studies. The topic of Christian theology and world religions merges into the topic of Christian theology and religious studies, and it is our conviction that we have shed new light on this topic within the pages of this book.

Our final word must be one of urgency. We have played our variations on the main theme, we have split the beam of light that is our topic into the colours of the rainbow, we have followed the canons of academic rigour in our approach to our subject. I hope too that through the webs of theological and religious debate there has shone through an emotional drive to convince the reader that *Christian Theology and World Religions: A Global Approach* is a topic whose hour has come. The *kairos* is now. Christian theology is changing to meet the global situation. Whether it can change fast enough to *create* the new situation rather than follow along in its wake depends upon whether the concerns we have demonstrated fully enter our bloodstream so that the Christian tradition and its theology can become truly global in our pulsating global world.

INDEX OF NAMES

Waardenburg, J. D. J., **17**, **71**
Warfield, B. B., **99**
Warren, M. A. C., 91
Watt, W. M., **71**
Whaling, F., **17**, **48**, **100**, **125f**, **143**
White, L. T., **143**

Wilhelm, H., **143**
Wright, A. F., **48**

Zaehner, R. C., **48**, 85f, **100**
Zimmer, H., **160**
Zoroaster, 21, 26, 48, 86

GENERAL INDEX

Absolute Reality, 89, 97, 113f, 116,
 119, 151
aesthetics
 common element in religions, 38f
 and religious studies, 129
African religion, 132–4, 173
American Indians, 140
anonymous Christians, 88
Axial age of religion, 25f, 28f, 31
Aztecs, 21, 32, 164

Baha'is, 34
Bangalore, Christian Institute, 92
Buddhism
 aesthetics, 46
 architecture, 46
 bliss, 46
 Bodhisattvas, 86
 Buddha, 25, 28f, 45–7, 86, 96
 Ch'an school, 138
 and China, 27f, 30f, 45, 130f,
 135f, 138f
 community, religious, 38, 45
 dharma (law), 39, 45–7, 63
 eightfold path, 46
 ethics, 45
 hand gestures, 46
 and humanity, 35
 and India, 28
 initiation ceremony, 45
 and Japan, 45
 lay role, 45
 Mahayana, 26–31, 38f, 45, 147
 meditation, 45f, 166
 monks, 38, 45
 mudras (hand gestures), 46
 mysticism, 31
 and nature, 35

Nirvana, 27, 46f, 63, 86, 98, 111
Noble Truths, four, 46
non-violence, 45
Pali Canon, 39, 45, 59
pluralism, 58, 63
political involvement, 32, 45
prayer, 45
Pure Land, 30f
and rebirth, 30, 39, 46
reform, 32
Refuges (pillars), three central,
 45
and revelation, 30
revival, 34
rise, 26, 29, 31
rituals, 45
transcendence, 35, 38, 46f
salvation, 46
sangha (monastic community),
 38, 45, 90
sculpture, 46
and social involvement, 39, 45
and SE Asia, 96, 177
spirituality, 46, 166
suffering, 46
Sutras, 39, 45
Theravada, 38f, 45, 147
and Trinity, 147
wheel, 46
and world, 30, 35, 46
Zen, 30, 138f

China
 and Buddhism, 27f, 30f, 45, 135f,
 138f
 and Confucianism, 21, 26–8, 30f,
 136–9
 and dialogue, inter-religious, 90

transcendence, 46f
and Trinity, 42, 147
worship, 42
Yahweh, 27, 47, 54, 89, 97, 111

knowledge
inner, 28
and theology, 120–2

liberation theology, 82, 136, 172
Logos, 85, 88, 116, 152, 159

McGill Institute of Islamic Studies, 103
Manichaean religion, 21, 164
Marxism *see* Communism
Mayas, 21, 32, 164
Mecca, 35, 40f
Medina, 35, 41
Mesopotamian religion, 21, 24–6, 164
monotheism, 23, 28, 39, 76
mystery religions, 55, 72, 75
mysticism, 31, 40f, 86, 115, 129, 152
myth, 25, 38f, 52f, 81, 128

Neolithic religion, 21, 23–5, 164

oikonomia, 128, 146

Palaeolithic religion, 21–4, 164
'passing over', spiritual technique, 129–31, 135f, 140f, 167f, 173f, 177f
Philosophia perennis school *see* philosophy, perennial
philosophy
and the Absolute, 89, 97, 113f, 116, 119, 128f, 147, 151
Greek, 75
Indian, 75
Ionian, 26, 29
perennial, 102, 112–24, 129, 178f
of religion, 60f
and sacraments, 55
and theology, 31, 51f, 60f

political involvement, common element in religions, 39
polytheism, 23, 75
presence theology, 90f
primal religions, 21, 34f, 135, 164f

relativistic theology, 64, 95–8
religions, history of, 21–37
religious dialogue, 35–7, 64, 89–95, 98f
religious studies
and Christian theology, 92, 102–25, 127–9, 179–81
and world religions, 168
religious tradition
evolution, 29
model for understanding, eightfold, 7
revelation, 30, 76–9, 104f
rites de passage, 38, 133
ritual, common element in religions, 38f

sacramental approach to God, 55, 75, 89
sacred kingship, 24
sacred texts, common element in religions, 38f
salvation
exclusivism, 74–6, 166f
and faith, 88
Fundamentals, 74f
and relativistic theology, 96
Roman Catholic dogma, 74
universalisation, 87–9
Sanskrit, 1, 30
science, modern, 35, 82, 133
sects and cults, modern, 164
secularisation, theological, 64, 79–83
Shintoism, 28
Sikhs, 21, 31
social involvement, common element in religions, 38f
spirituality
among Chinese Christians, 137f
common element in religions, 38, 40, 179

and dialogue, 93f
and *philosophia perennis* school,
115, 117, 123f
Western lack, present-day, 152
Stoics, 50f, 54f, 57
symbolism, religious, 34, 128, 133

Tao Fong Shan, 135f
Taoism
and China, 21, 27f, 30, 135,
137–9
and Christ, 86
humility, 86
influence diminished, present-
day, 34
and Japan, 21, 28
origins, 26
Tao, 86, 98
and Trinity, 147
theologia
academic study, 59
Bible, not in, 53f
Christian use, 53–70
development of word, 49–70
and doctrine, 58, 60, 69
and Greeks, 49f, 55, 68f, 169
Hebrew, corresponding terms,
54
and *humanitas*, 52, 57f, 68f, 120f
and mythology, 51
modern use, 62–70
Patristic use, 55–8, 146
and philosophy, 51f
and Reformers, 62, 69
and Roman Catholic Church,
62
and Roman world, 50, 68, 169
Scholastic use, 58–62
and Stoics, 50, 54f, 57
and transcendence, 51, 53, 69
and Trinity, 57, 69, 128, 146
theology (*see also* Christian
theology)
black, 172
of comparative religion, 11
and dialogue, 64, 89–95
feminine, 156, 172
and liberal arts, 52

in multi-religious situation,
63–7, 106f
and natural science, 66
and philosophy, 50–2, 60f
and plural disciplines, 65f, 111
process, 172
queen of sciences, 60, 66, 120
and religious studies, 92, 102–25
and revelation, 61, 64f
systematic, 59, 62, 128
term, 10, 49–70, 169f, 180
and Trinity, 16
and world religions, 12, 16, 63f,
106–10, 170
transcendence
in Buddhism, 35, 46
in Chinese religion, 35, 137, 139f,
177
Christian view, 16, 35, 46, 177
and faith, 88, 106
global awareness, 35, 115, 165
God the Father, 151, 153
in Greek world, 50
in Hinduism, 35, 46f, 148
in Islam, 41, 46
in major religions, 7f, 10, 27, 46,
103, 166
in Neolithic religion, 23f
and origin of religions, 116
in Palaeolithic religion, 23
and *philosophia perennis* school,
118f, 123f, 129
in primal religion, 23, 35, 164
and reality, 104
in religious studies, 111
and theology, 69, 115, 118
Trinity, 177
and unity of religions, 115–17
Trinity
and Confucianism, 147
and Indian religion, 145–59,
177
and Islam, 147
and Judaism, 42, 147
key to theology, 16
male and female aspects, 156–9
and New Testament, 54
patristic theology, 59